SAP Legacy System Migration Workbench (LSMW)

Antje Kunz

Antje Kunz:
SAP ® Legacy System Migration Workbench (LSMW)

ISBN:	978-1502786265
Editors:	Anja Achilles
Translation:	Tracey Duffy
Coverdesign:	Philip Esch, Martin Munzel
Cover Photo:	Fotolia: #40519306 © S.John
Interior Design:	Johann-Christian Hanke
Layout:	1-2-buch.de, M. Albrecht

All rights reserved.
1st Edition 2014, Gleichen
© Espresso Tutorials GmbH
URL: www.espresso-tutorials.com

Neither this publication nor any part of it may be copied or reproduced in any form or by any means or translated into another language without the prior consent of Espresso Tutorials GmbH, Zum Gelenberg 11, 37130 Gleichen, Germany.

Espresso Tutorials makes no warranties or representations with respects to the content hereof and specifically disclaims any implied warranties of merchantability or fitness for any particular purpose. Espresso Tutorials assumes no responsibility for any errors that may appear in this publication.

Feedback

We greatly appreciate any kind of feedback you have concerning this book. Please mail us at info@espresso-tutorials.com!

Content

1	Introduction	7
2	**Overview of the Legacy System Migration Workbench (LSMW)**	**11**
	2.1 Areas of Application	11
	2.2 System Prerequisites and Authorizations	13
	2.3 Starting LSMW	15
	2.4 The LSMW Initial Screen	16
	2.5 Creating a Project	17
	2.6 Buttons and Central Functions	19
3	**Data Migration**	**23**
	3.1 LSMW Main Menu	24
	3.1.1 Execute	25
	3.1.2 User Menu	25
	3.1.3 Numbering On/Off	26
	3.1.4 Double-Click = Display/Change	27
	3.1.5 Object Overview	27
	3.1.6 Action Log	27
	3.2 Maintaining Object Attributes	28
	3.3 Maintaining Source Structures	33
	3.4 Maintaining Source Fields	35
	3.5 Maintaining Structure Relationships	39
	3.8 Maintaining Field Mapping and Conversion Rules	42
	3.7 Maintaining Fixed Values, Translations, and User-Defined Routines	56
	3.8 Specifying Files	62
	3.9 Assigning Files	68
	3.10 Importing Files	69
	3.11 Displaying Imported Data	71
	3.12 Converting Data	72

	3.13	Displaying Converted Data	74
	3.14	Creating Batch Input Sessions	76
	3.15	Processing Batch Input Sessions	79
	3.16	Object Overview	83

4 Recordings — 87

4.1	Creating Recordings	88
4.2	Using the Recording Import Technology in the LSMW	97

5 LSMW Using BAPI and IDoc Import Technology — 107

5.1	General Definitions	108
5.2	Basic Settings for Using BAPIs and IDocs	109
5.3	Creating Orders Using the BAPI Technology	114

6 Long Texts — 127

6.1	Long Texts in SAP	127
6.2	LSMW Objects for Long Texts	129
6.3	Long Texts — Source Structures, Source Fields, Structure Relationships	132
6.4	Long Text — Field Mapping	133
6.5	Final Process Steps for Transferring Long Texts	136

7 Transporting Projects — 139

7.1	Transport via Change Request	139
7.2	Exporting Projects	140
7.3	Importing Projects	141

8   Additional Information   **143**

    8.1   Periodic Data Transfer   143
    8.2   Global Functions and Variables   147
    8.3   Display Variants and Processing Times   149
    8.4   Suppressing Data Records   152
    8.5   Creating Additional Data Records   153

9   Closing Words   **157**

A   The Author   **160**

B   Index   **161**

C   Disclaimer   **166**

More books from Espresso Tutorials   **165**

1 Introduction

Do you want to migrate data, make mass changes to existing data, transfer data from non-SAP systems to SAP systems without having to do any programming, etc.?

Are you looking for a tool that you can use to do all of this effectively and in the standard SAP system, without needing any additional components and software?

Welcome to the Legacy System Migration Workbench — hereinafter referred to as LSMW or LSM Workbench.

This book will explain the possibilities that LSMW offers and will show you step-by-step how these options can help you to migrate data successfully. You will learn the areas of application that LSMW is designed for and the prerequisites that have to be fulfilled to use the LSM Workbench, such as any SAP authorizations required, etc.

The main focus of this book is on providing a good understanding of how LSMW works. To achieve this objective, it uses practical examples that are easy to understand and numerous illustrations. It offers users who have no previous experience with LSMW a good introduction to the topic. Experienced users will also find this book valuable as a reference work and will undoubtedly also learn something.

In the book, I will look at the various import methods that LSMW offers in detail and explain each of them using an example. One chapter is dedicated specifically to migrating long texts.

You will learn how to create recordings of SAP transactions and then use them to load and change data using LSMW.

I will show you how to structure and find LSM Workbenches and explain the important issues for administration of the workbench.

You will also learn some tricks for working with the LSM Workbench: for example, how to export and import an LSMW and how to skip or duplicate data records during imports.

In the section "Additional Information," experienced LSMW users will probably experience one or two "light bulb moments."

The examples used in this book were created in the IDES environment in SAP Release ECC 6.0. Many thanks to consolut for allowing me to use this system.

I hope you will enjoy reading and working with the book!

In the text, boxes are used to highlight important information. Each box also has an icon to identify it more precisely:

Notes offer practical tips for dealing with the respective topic.

Warnings draw your attention to possible sources of error or stumbling blocks in connection with a topic.

Finally, a note concerning the copyright: All screenshots printed in this book are the copyright of SAP AG. All rights are reserved by SAP AG. Copyright pertains to all SAP images in this publication. For simplification, we will not mention this specifically underneath every screenshot.

2 Overview of the Legacy System Migration Workbench (LSMW)

In this chapter, you will learn about the areas of application for LSMW and what exactly *Legacy System Migration Workbench* means. You will also learn about the support this tool offers and what its core functions are.

The Legacy System Migration Workbench (LSMW) is part of the SAP system and has been included in the standard SAP system since Basis Release ERP 6.0. You can use this integrated development environment to migrate external data (from non-SAP systems) and to perform mass updates within existing SAP systems.

LSMW is a cross-application (CA) component of the SAP system. Its use is not specific to any platform, and it has interfaces to the Data Transfer Center, to batch input (BTCI), and direct input processing, as well as to the standard interfaces BAPI and IDoc.

From a historical perspective, the LSM Workbench is based on the standard tool for migration from SAP R/2 to SAP R/3.

2.1 Areas of Application

You can use the LSM Workbench to migrate both simple and complex data, referred to in the SAP context as *source structures*.

The advantages of the LSM Workbench are particularly beneficial if you want to migrate legacy data whose structures are very different to the structures in SAP, meaning that you have to convert data.

However, the LSM Workbench is not only useful for migrations and new implementations; it can also be very helpful in a live SAP system. The technology is particularly useful if you want to make changes to user-specific fields but cannot perform these changes using the mass change transactions (e.g., MASS, XD99, XK99).

The LSM Workbench is used to migrate external data to SAP, that is, from *legacy systems* to R/3. You can perform this data transfer as a one-time transfer or at recurring periodic intervals. Within the LSMW tool, you can also convert data.

The following SAP standard methods are available for importing external or legacy data to SAP using LSMW:

▶ Batch input

▶ Direct input

▶ IDocs

▶ BAPIs

We will look at the individual functions in more detail in Chapters 4 to 6 with extensive examples.

The sequence of the data migration using LSMW, starting from importing one or more files up to transfer into the SAP system, is shown in figure 2.1. The core functions of the LSM Workbench are:

▶ Read in data from the legacy system

▶ Convert data into SAP format

▶ Import data into the SAP database

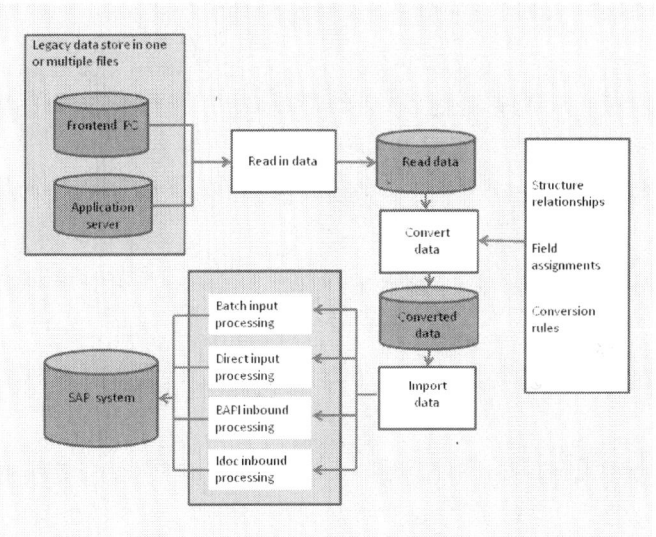

Figure 2.1: Central functions of LSMW

2.2 System Prerequisites and Authorizations

The system prerequisite for using the LSM Workbench is SAP Basis Release 4.0 or higher. However, LSMW is not included in the standard SAP delivery scope until Basis Release 6.20, meaning R/3 Enterprise, ERP 2004, ECC 6.0, and higher versions. If you want to use LSMW in an older release, you have to install this SAP functionality first via a transport request. You can download this free of charge from SAP Service Marketplace (https://service.sap.com/lsmw).

The logistical prerequisite for successful data migration with LSMW is completion of the Customizing in the target SAP system. It must be possible to process the relevant transactions manually without any errors: this means that you can only use LSMW when you have installed the SAP system and completed the application Customizing.

To determine which fields have to be filled in the target system, you should first run the processes that you want to migrate data for with test data from the legacy system. This will indicate quickly whether data from the legacy system can be delivered for all SAP required fields. If this is not the case, you should consult users from the corresponding specialist departments to agree on a standard value to be defined in LSMW.

Before starting the LSMW work, it is important to be clear about which fields are to be transferred 1:1 from the legacy system, which fields require translation, and where you will have to program conversion logic. You should document these analyses in writing so that you can refer to them at any time during the migration project.

As you can use the LSMW to change and/or supplement the data in SAP, an authorization concept is defined for checking access authorization. This means that to use the LSM Workbench, special authorizations are required, and these are subdivided into the following four profiles (see Table 2.1):

Authorization level	Profile	Function
Display	B_LSMW_SHOW	The user can display all projects together with their process steps. He cannot switch to change mode.
Execute	B_LSMW_EXEC	The user can display, read in, convert, and import data.
Change	B_LSMW_CHG	The user has "Execute" authorization and can thus change and copy objects.
Administration	B_LSMW_ALL	The user can use all of the functions that the tool provides.

Table 2.1: Authorization profiles in LSMW

2.3 Starting LSMW

You start the Legacy System Migration Workbench by calling up SAP transaction LSMW. This is not a transaction that is already defined in the SAP menu. Via the menu path FAVORITES • INSERT TRANSACTION, add transaction LSMW to your favorites (see Figure 2.2).

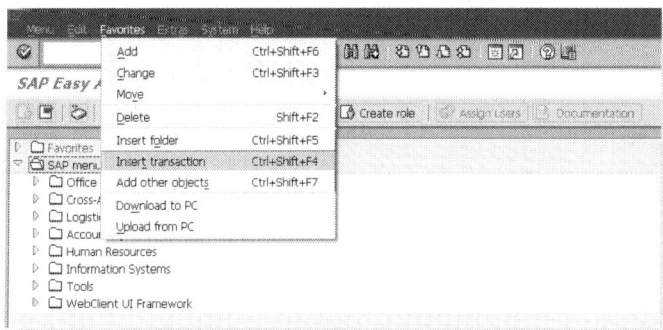

Figure 2.2: Adding favorites 1

As soon as you have entered the required transaction LSMW and confirmed with ENTER, you can call up the LSM Workbench on the SAP initial screen.

You can also call up transaction LSMW at any time via the command field.

The first time you call up this transaction, a welcome screen appears (see Figure 2.3).

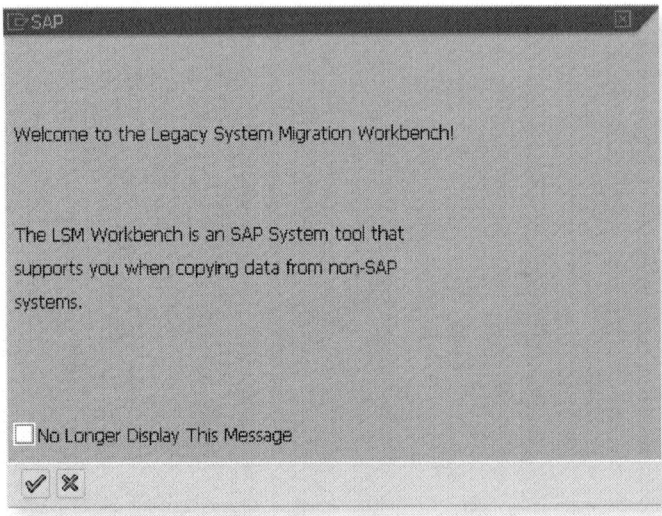

Figure 2.3: LSMW welcome screen 1

If you select ☑ No Longer Display This Message, this information is no longer displayed in future and the LSMW initial screen appears immediately.

2.4 The LSMW Initial Screen

The LSMW initial screen (see Figure 2.4) shows the structured layout of the data migration objects, divided into:

- Project
- Subproject
- Object

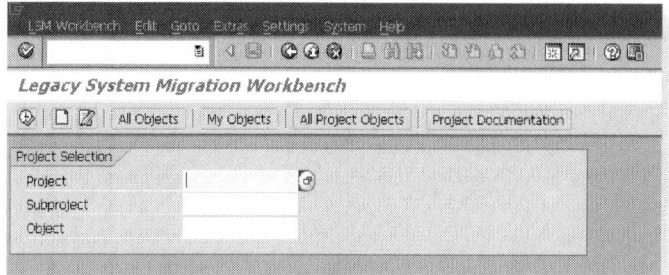

Figure 2.4: LSMW initial screen

Here you can create new projects complete with substructures or parts of projects or search for existing migration objects.

It is highly recommended that, together with the members of the project, you agree on a joint, easily understandable structure at the beginning of the data migration.

2.5 Creating a Project

A project, also referred to as a *migration object*, represents a data unit and can contain an unlimited number of subprojects. You can choose any (maximum 15-character) code as the project name, for example: "AK-Migration."

As already stated, you should address the properties of your migration project during the structuring. For example, if you have to migrate data from various systems, you can create different projects to make it easier to assign the data clearly. However, it does not make sense to create an

17

infinite number of very small projects as this can lead to difficulties in finding the projects later on.

Unfortunately, there is no standard guideline for structuring, but Chapter 3 contains some useful examples.

In the DESCRIPTION field, you can enter a more detailed description of the project up to a maximum of 60 characters (including spaces).

You create a new project by positioning the cursor on the PROJECT field and clicking CREATE ENTRY ( ) (see Figure 2.5).

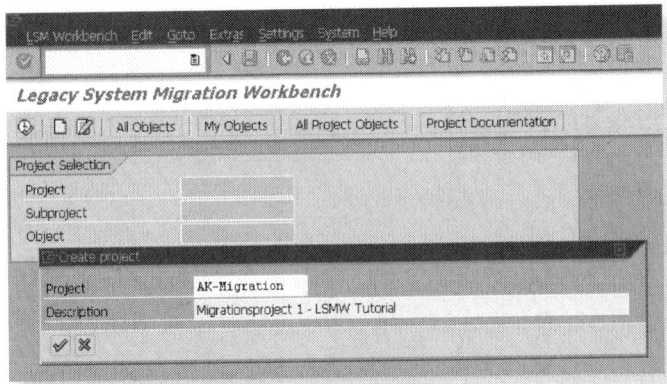

Figure 2.5: Creating an LSMW project

In the same way that a project can consist of any number of subprojects, the subproject can in turn consist of any number of objects.

If you want to create a complete LSMW project, you must also enter information for these two data units. Here too, you can use a 15-character code for the name of the subproject and object, and you can enter an additional, maximum 60-character description.

Selecting a good structure makes it easier to find and reuse existing objects later.

Figure 2.6 and Figure 2.7 show the creation of an object and subproject and the finished name of the new LMSW.

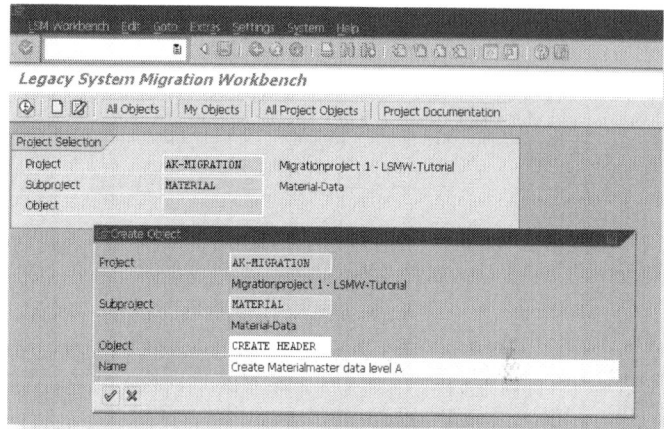

Figure 2.6: Creating an LSMW object

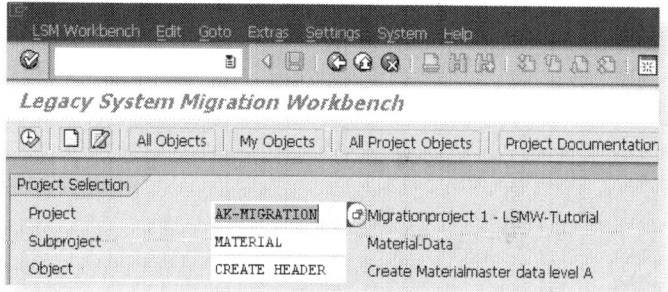

Figure 2.7: Creating an LSMW project

2.6 Buttons and Central Functions

The LSMW initial screen offers some useful buttons and functions (see Figure 2.8) that we will look at more closely below.

OVERVIEW OF THE LSMW

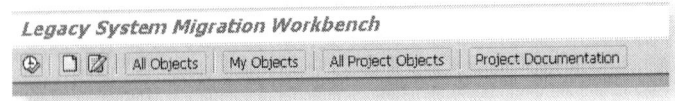

Figure 2.8: LMSW administration screen

▶ ALL OBJECTS provides an overview of the existing projects, subprojects, and objects in the system, including the owners and names.

▶ MY OBJECTS shows all objects created under your current user ID. However, at least one LSMW process step must have been executed for the owner to be recognized and the object displayed.

▶ ALL PROJECT OBJECTS shows all available objects for the selected project in a tree structure (see Figure 2.9).

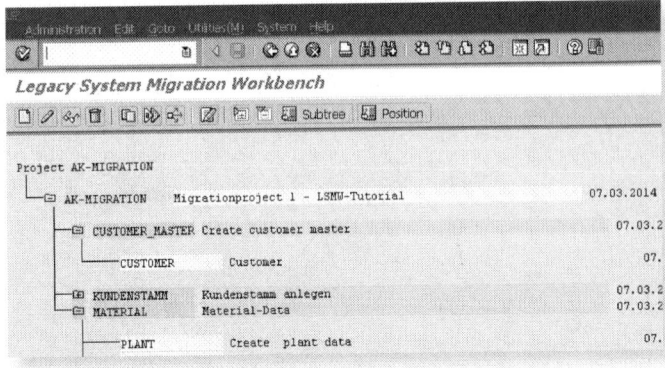

Figure 2.9: LSMW project overview 1

In this view, provided you have the relevant authorization (see Table 2.1), you can make changes, as well as delete and rename objects, subprojects, and projects.

If you want to list all projects in the tree structure, set the PROJECTS field on the initial screen to *space* (blank) and then click ALL PROJECT OBJECTS. The view then switches to the LSM WORKBENCH ADMINISTRATION, which we will look at in more detail below.

► Project Documentation shows the entire documentation that you have created for the individual project steps. You can print this documentation, save it in different formats, or send it.

► Using the Documentation button, you can create notes for any previously selected structure object. These cannot be translated with the usual SAP tools and are only available in the language in which they are maintained. In an international project, you should therefore agree on a common language (usually English) beforehand.

► You use the Create Entry button to create a new project.

As the name already indicates, the Administration function offers extensive LSMW administration options. You can access this function via the menu path Goto • Administration (see Figure 2.10).

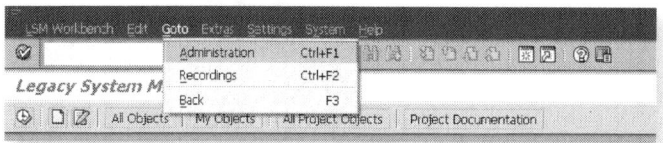

Figure 2.10: Administration

Here, all of the projects created in the LSM Workbench are displayed in a structured form, together with the subproject(s) and object(s). Figure 2.11 also shows the reusable rules, that is, fixed values, translations, and user-defined routines that we will look at in more detail in Section 3.7.

OVERVIEW OF THE LSMW

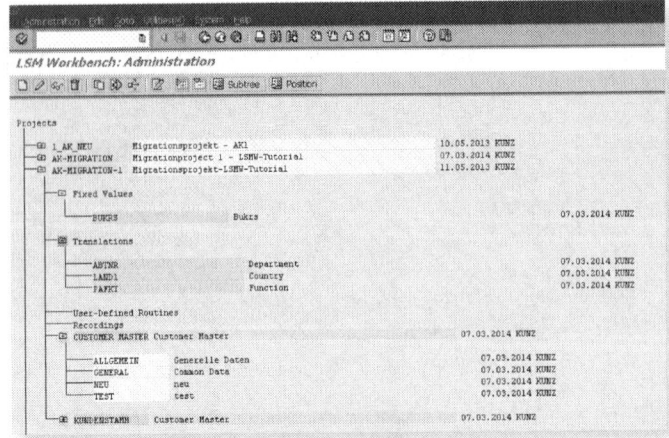

Figure 2.11: Administration — detail

In the LSMW administration area, you can create, search for, display, edit, rename, copy, and delete objects (Figure 2.12).

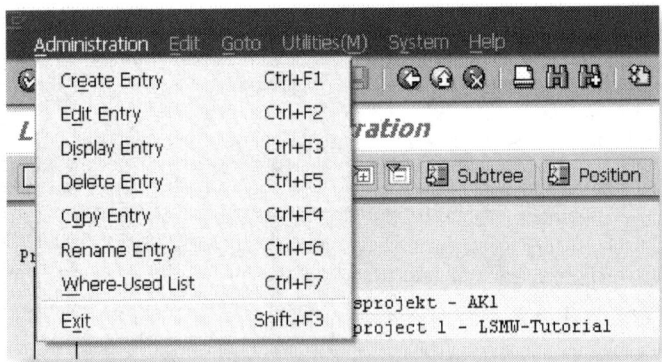

Figure 2.12: Administration — functions

All changes are logged with the change date, time, and user name of the person who executed the last change.

You can look at these change logs in the action log (Action Log) of the LSMW user guidance screen (see Section 3.1.6) and reset them if necessary.

22

3 Data Migration

This is the most important chapter in the book — the actual data migration. Step-by-step, I will demonstrate the work processes required for transferring data to the SAP system using LSMW. I will illustrate this using a practical example from logistics. At the end of this section, you should be able to develop your own LSMW project.

In our example, we begin with the migration of the customer master data. We assume that the relevant data has already been extracted from the source system and is available in Excel format. For each customer (referred to as "debitor" in our example), there is a header record with the corresponding master information and (multiple) item records depending on the number of contact persons defined for the customer in the legacy system.

Extracts for the two Excel files for our example are shown in Figure 3.1 and Figure 3.2:

	A	B	C	D	E	F	G
1	debitor	country	name	place	postal code	phone	street
2	200000	GER	Udo Neureich	Gunzenhausen	91710	09831-45678	Goldanger 99
3	210000	GER	Maria Magnicht	Dresden	04244	04442-123000	Flowerstreet 8
4	220000	GER	Lilo Lichtblick	Frankfurt	60433	069-9874560	Hill 5
5	230000	GER	Norbert Neureich	Tegernsee	83684	08022-00047	Paradise 7
6	240000	GER	Olaf Obenauf	Hamburg	15938	035452-4545	Castle place 11
7	250000	GER	Max Garden	Frankfurt	09526	037360-456789	Street number 6
8	260000	USA	Billy Gutes AG	Chicago, IL	60637	773-702-7777	Michigan Avenue 444

Figure 3.1: Debitor header file

23

DATA MIGRATION

	A	B	C	D	E	F	G
2	200000	Ms.	Maria	Singer	purchasing	purchasing	303-126-951
3	200000	Mr.	Bruce	Reed	sales	sales	303-126-929
4	210000	Ms.	Kathleen	Mitchell	purchasing	purchasing director	(07808) 575-166
5	210000	Mr.	Greg	Riker	sales	sales director	(07808) 575-150
6	210000	Mr.	Alan	Miller	security	director security	(07808) 575-177
7	210000	Ms.	Teresa	Sales	purchasing	purchasing assistant	(07808) 575-100
8	220000	Ms.	Kate	Newman	sales	sales	069-98745611
9	220000	Mr.	Roy	Swift	sales	sales director	069-98745620

header-data contact-person

Figure 3.2: Debitor contact person file

As stated in Section 2.5, here I will present a possible structure for the entire migration project (see also Figure 3.3):

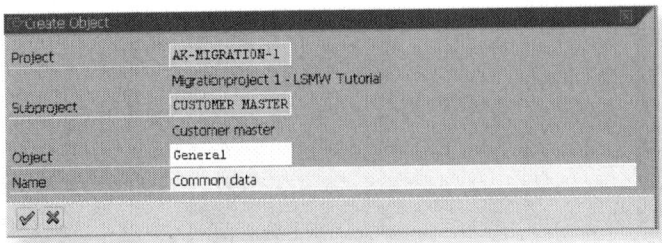

Figure 3.3: LSMW example project

Using this project structure, we will now start to create the LMSW and to do so, we turn to the main menu of the LSM Workbench.

3.1 LSMW Main Menu

Now that you have learned how to create and manage a project with subproject(s) and objects in Chapter 2, click EXECUTE (⊕) (see Figure 2.6) to proceed to the LSMW main menu (user guidance screen), shown in Figure 3.4, which I refer to repeatedly in the following sections of Chapter 3.

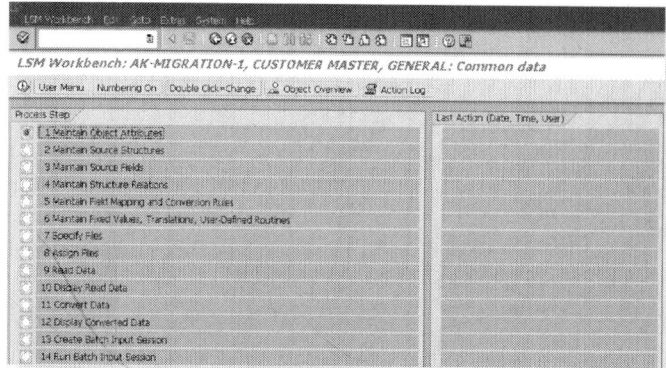

Figure 3.4: LSMW main menu

I will address the functions available in this main menu briefly in the following six sections.

3.1.1 Execute

When you select a process step with the selection button (⦿), click EXECUTE ( ) or double-click the selected entry to start the process step.

3.1.2 User Menu

Figure 3.5 shows the user menu that you have personalized to your requirements by selecting all process steps that should be displayed for you.

DATA MIGRATION

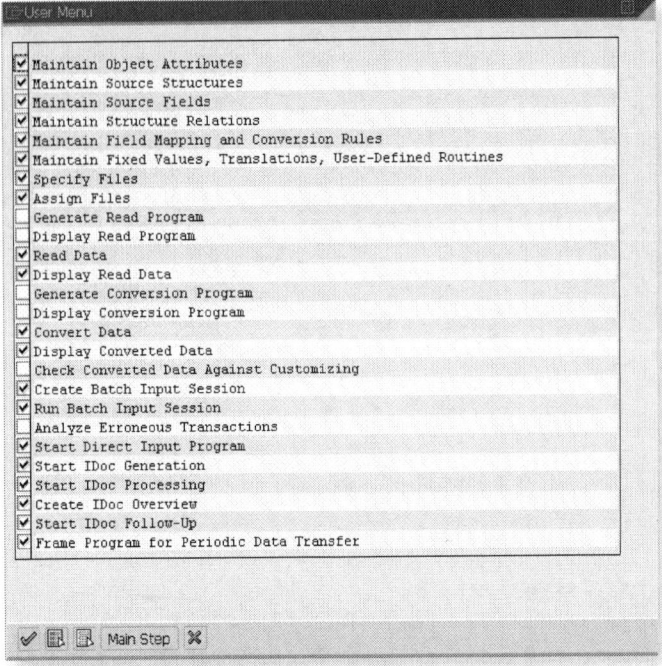

Figure 3.5: LSMW — user menu

This can be an advantage if you have already executed certain process steps and do not want them to be displayed again for selection. You can reset these settings at any time and you can activate all necessary process steps automatically by selecting the MAIN STEP function.

3.1.3 Numbering On/Off

You can use this function to switch the numbering of the individual menu items on or off.

3.1.4 Double-Click = Display/Change

Here you can define whether you want to switch to change or display mode with a DOUBLE-CLICK when processing the individual menu items. This can be an advantage as a default setting to save switching between display and change in the respective menu item. For our example below, we choose DOUBLE-CLICK = CHANGE here.

3.1.5 Object Overview

This function gives you a complete overview for the selected object, either in list or table form. All translations, reusable rules, and fixed values used in the object are displayed. At the beginning of the LSMW creation this overview is empty. Therefore, we will look at this overview again more closely in Section 3.16.

3.1.6 Action Log

The action log logs all measures executed in the project, with date, user name, time, and corresponding process steps. You can delete change logs created under your user ID from the overview via EXTRAS - RESET ACTION LOG. This measure is also logged as the process step "Reset Action Log," with name, date, and time.

We will now execute the individual process steps of the LSMW main menu (see Figure 3.4).

3.2 Maintaining Object Attributes

The maintenance of the attributes is the first process step of the LSM Workbench. Here you define the type of file transfer, the object type, and the import method. Double-click MAINTAIN OBJECT ATTRIBUTES in the LSMW main menu (see Figure 3.4) to navigate to the corresponding selection screen (see Figure 3.6):

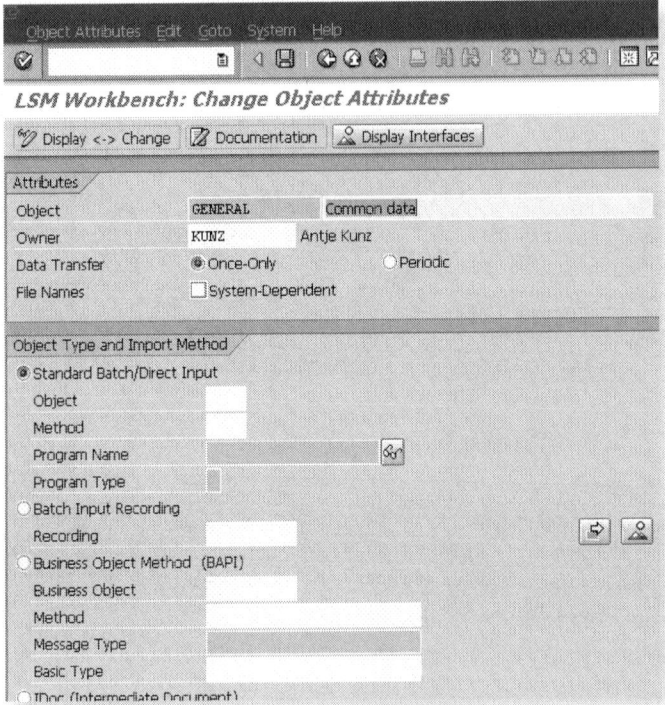

Figure 3.6: Maintaining object attributes

In Section 3.1.4, we set the function DOUBLE-CLICK=CHANGE. This means that we are immediately in change mode. However, you can change this mode at any time via the DISPLAY <-> CHANGE function.

In the top part of the screen, ATTRIBUTES, the entries OBJECT and OWNER already contain the information from the project we created in Chapter 3.

You can also change the owner and the object name here. It may make sense to change the owner if you are collaborating in larger work groups and different process steps within an LSMW are to be executed by different people. The person entered here will easily find the corresponding LSMW under MY OBJECTS (see Section 2.6).

In this section, you also configure whether the data transfer is to be a once-only transfer or a periodic transfer. For our example, we choose the ONCE-ONLY data transfer and thus define that we want to use the object for a once-only transfer of data from an existing system (legacy system) to R/3. In this case, you can load data that is on the frontend (i.e., your PC).

In a PERIODIC DATA TRANSFER, the expectation is that data will be read from the R/3 application server. We will look at this special technology more closely in Section 8.1.

In the ATTRIBUTES section, you can also define whether the file names should be maintained on a system-dependent basis. If you select this field, you can specify a separate file name for each SAP system later under SPECIFY FILES. This is very useful if you want to migrate data into multiple SAP systems.

We will now look at the second area on the object attributes screen: OBJECT TYPE AND IMPORT METHOD. As mentioned in Section 2.1, here you have access to four import methods.

For our example we choose the import method STANDARD BATCH/DIRECT INPUT and using the F4 INPUT HELP, the relevant object CUSTOMER MASTER (0050) (see Figure 3.7).

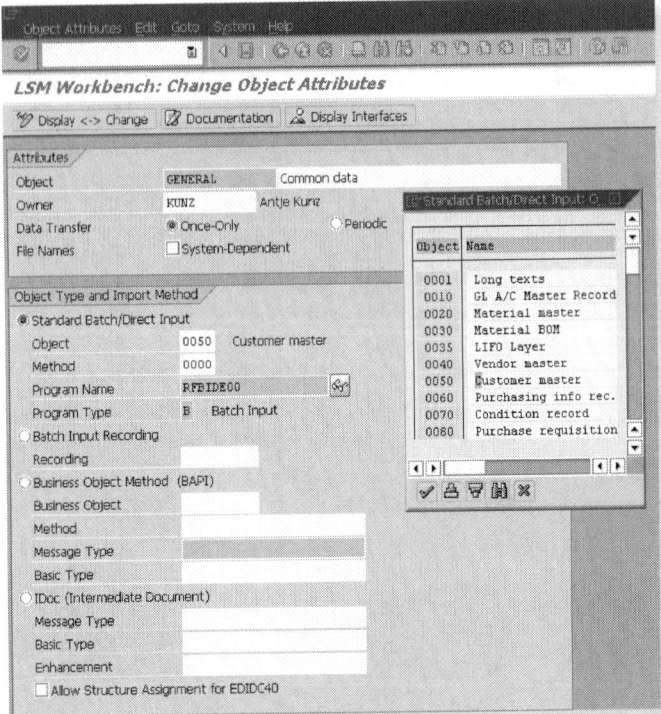

Figure 3.7: LSMW — object selection

The SAP system stipulates the program name (RFBIDE00) and program type (B = batch input) for our selection. For more information about this program, use the DISPLAY function ( ) to navigate directly to the ABAP Editor initial screen (see Figure 3.8). There you can display the source code and the program documentation.

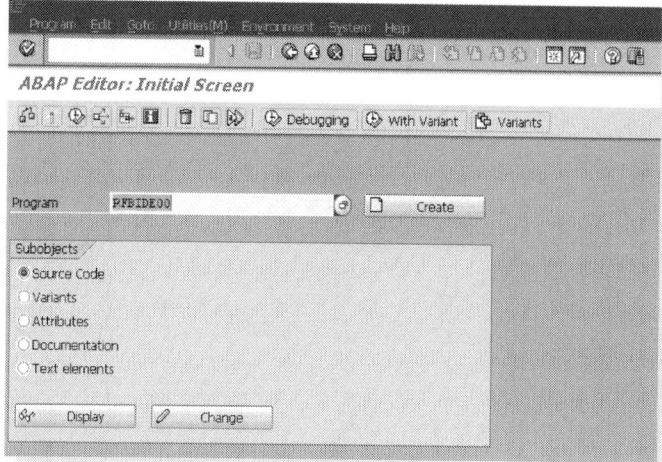

Figure 3.8: ABAP Editor, RFBIDE00

The LSM Workbench supports various import technologies with SAP standard interfaces.

You can display a selection of the import method(s) for the respective import technology by calling up the available interfaces via the [Display Interfaces] function. In our case, the SAP system proposes the use of batch input for the migration of the customer master data (see Figure 3.9, method 1 and 2):

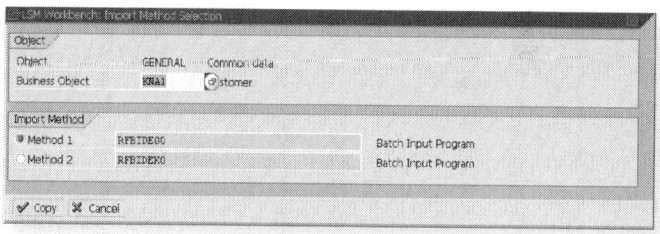

Figure 3.9: LSMW — selecting the import method

Once we have completed all of the entries on this screen, they are saved and we return to the overview of all LSMW process steps.

31

It makes sense to use the import technology offered by SAP dependent on the data object. The following is an extract of the existing SAP standard interfaces for each business object:

- Material master: direct input
- Customer and vendor: batch input
- Business partner: IDoc
- HR master data: batch input

You can use the following criteria to decide which import technology is most suitable for your business object:

Availability: not all import technologies are available for every data object. Check in advance which SAP standard interfaces are available.

Data volume: if the volume of data to be migrated is large, runtime problems can occur. In this case, direct input is preferred over batch input processing.

User-friendliness: as you will see below, the batch input technology has very good options for error analysis and postprocessing missing data.

Difficulty: if your legacy data has a very simple structure, or you only want to change a limited number of fields and the related SAP transactions always deliver the same screen sequence, you can use the *recording technology*.

3.3 Maintaining Source Structures

We will now look at the second process step in the LSM Workbench, which we access by double-clicking MAINTAIN SOURCE STRUCTURES in the LSMW main menu (see Figure 3.4). The following selection window appears (see Figure 3.10):

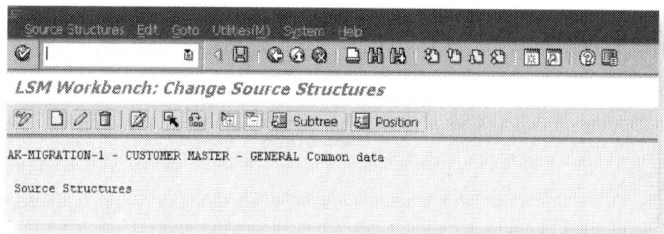

Figure 3.10: Maintaining source structures 1

You define the source structures by entering the structure name (name of the source structure), the structure description (explanatory text), and the hierarchical relationship.

To create a source structure, position the cursor on SOURCE STRUCTURES and select CREATE STRUCTURE ( ). For our example, we create a structure with the name HEAD and the description COMMON CUSTOMER MASTER. Click ENTER or CONTINUE ( ) to return to the LSM WORKBENCH: CHANGE SOURCE STRUCTURES screen. If you need additional structures, place the cursor on the structure you have already created and choose CREATE STRUCTURE again. A dialog box appears, asking whether the structure should be at the same level or at a lower level (see Figure 3.11).

DATA MIGRATION

> **Hierarchy of the Source Structure**
>
>  When creating a source structure, always start with the highest hierarchy level as you can only add structures at the same level or lower levels.

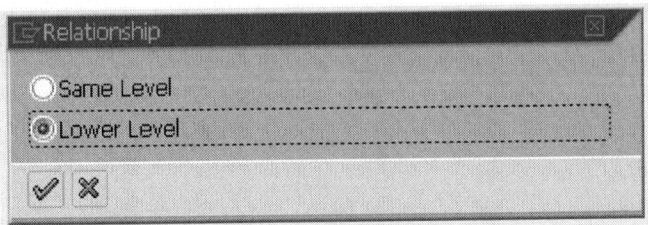

Figure 3.11: Maintaining source structures 2

We choose LOWER LEVEL and in the next dialog box, enter the name CONTACT and the description CONTACT PERSON AT CUSTOMER. Figure 3.12 shows the result.

> **Recordings**
>
>  User-specific objects, that is, objects created using the recording technology, have a flat target structure. You only have to define one structure for these objects. For more details, see Chapter 4, "Recordings."

34

DATA MIGRATION

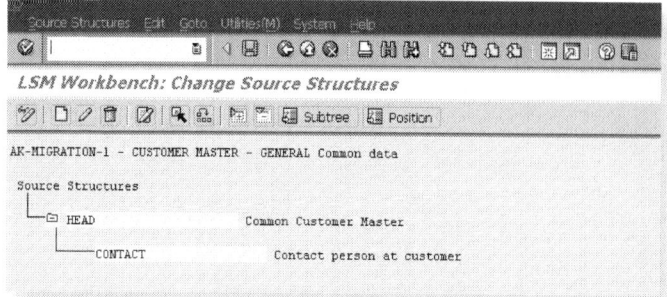

Figure 3.12: Maintaining source structures 3

In this process step, you can also use the ☐ ⌀ 🗑 ⌸ ⚒ ⚙ buttons to create, change, delete, or reassign source structures.

3.4 Maintaining Source Fields

Now that we have created the source structures, we maintain the related source fields. In the LSMW main menu (see Figure 3.4), click the corresponding area to access the MAINTAIN SOURCE FIELDS process step. The initial screen is very similar to Figure 3.12.

The source fields to be created result from the legacy data to be migrated and must be set up with the corresponding field structure. For our example (see Figure 3.1 and Figure 3.2), this means that for the source structure HEAD, we define the fields DEBITOR, COUNTRY, NAME, PLACE, etc., and for the source structure CONTACT, the fields DEBITOR, TITLE, NAME, etc.

You can create the source fields individually or in the form of a table. In our example, we create them individually. Place the cursor on the relevant source structure (here HEAD) and choose CREATE FIELD (☐). The following dialog box appears (see Figure 3.13):

35

DATA MIGRATION

Figure 3.13: Creating source fields 1

Under FIELD NAME, enter the corresponding name. You can enter any description you choose. As standard, the system proposes field length 10 and field type C (character field). Twenty further field type options are available via the F4 input help (🗔). Choose the relevant field definitions.

Step-by-step, we create the source fields for our example structures HEAD and CONTACT. Figure 3.14 shows the result.

Note that a new field is always entered below the original cursor position.

> **Identifying Field Content**
>
> If a file contains data for multiple source structures, the value of the relevant source structure must be specified under IDENTIFYING FIELD CONTENT.
> Identifying field content may only be specified for <u>one</u> field for each source structure.

If you want to conduct a migration test with a limited volume of data, for a field of the top hierarchy level (in our example, fields of the source structure HEAD), select ☐ Selection Parameter for "Import/Convert Data". This field is normally used for tests to enable a restriction of the volume of data to be read in at field level. For our example, we select this parameter in the DEBITOR field of the source structure HEAD (see also Figure 3.14).

```
Source Fields  Edit  Goto  Utilities(M)  System  Help

LSM Workbench: Change Source Fields

                                        Subtree   Position   Fields with the Same Name

AK-MIGRATION-1 - CUSTOMER MASTER - GENERAL Common data

Source Fields
  └─ HEAD                    Common Customer Master
      ├─ DEBITOR              C(006)    Debitor
      │                                 Selection Parameter for "Import/Convert Data"
      ├─ COUNTRY              C(003)    Country
      ├─ NAME                 C(030)    Name
      ├─ PLACE                C(030)    Place
      ├─ P_CODE               C(005)    Postal Code
      ├─ PHONE                C(015)    Phone
      ├─ STREET               C(030)    street
      └─ CONTACT              Contact person at customer
          ├─ DEBITOR          C(006)    Debitor
          ├─ TITEL            C(004)    Titel
          ├─ F_NAME           C(030)    First name
          ├─ L_NAME           C(030)    Last name
          ├─ DEPARTMENT       C(010)    Department
          ├─ ROLE             C(020)    Role at customer
          └─ PHONE            C(010)    Phone number at customer
```

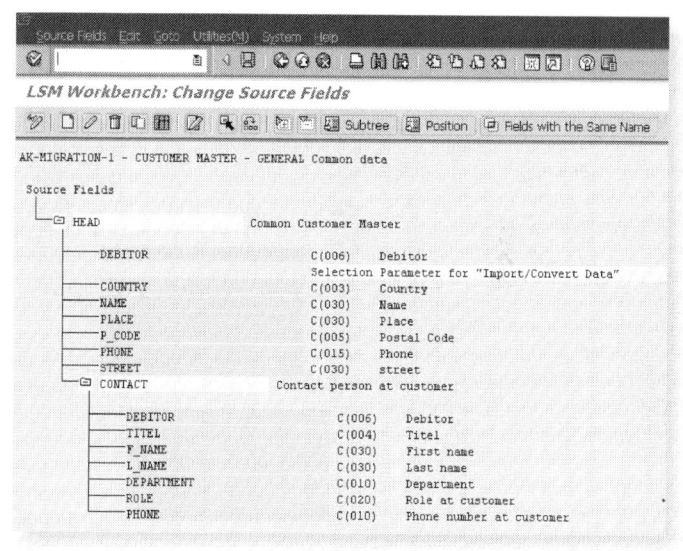

Figure 3.14: Creating source fields 2

As already stated, you can also maintain the source fields in the form of a table. To do this, place the cursor on a source structure or a source field that you have already created and select TABLE MAINTENANCE (▦). The overview shown in Figure 3.15 appears. Enter the FIELD NAME, TYPE, LENGTH, and FIELD DESCRIPTION.

If you only enter the field name and then choose ENTER, the system assigns the following values:

37

- Field Type: C
- Field Length: 10
- Field Description: as the field name

You can change/overwrite these values at any time.

If there is a domain in the SAP system whose name matches the field name entered, the domain name is automatically suggested as the field description.

Source Fields for Source Structure HEAD

Field Name	Type	Le..	Field description
DEBITOR	C	6	Debitor
COUNTRY	C	3	Country
NAME	C	30	Name
PLACE	C	30	Place
P_CODE	C	5	Postal Code
PHONE	C	15	Phone
STREET	C	30	street

Figure 3.15: Creating source fields 3

If you click FIELDS WITH THE SAME NAME, all source fields that occur more than once are displayed. This enables you to clearly see the key fields of dependent structures (see Figure 3.14, field DEBITOR). You can also see whether there are matching names in different source structures. In this case, you should change these names so that all non-key fields in the source structures are always unique.

3.5 Maintaining Structure Relationships

In Section 3.3, we created the source structures. In this process step, we will look at the target structures and establish the structure relationships between our project and the SAP system.

In the LSMW main menu (see Figure 3.4), choose the process step MAINTAIN STRUCTURE RELATIONSHIPS. A screen appears, showing the structures already used in the SAP system (see Figure 3.16). There you can see which target structures must be filled (in our example, BGR00, BKN00, and BKNA1). The target structures are dependent on the selected object attributes. In our example, with the selection of the import technology for the object CUSTOMER MASTER (see Figure 3.7), we have implicitly defined that the data must be provided in a format that can be processed by batch input program RFBIDE00.

I will now show you how to create a structure relationship. Position the cursor on the code for an SAP structure (beginning with BGR00) and choose CREATE RELATIONSHIP (Relationship). A dialog box opens, displaying the source structures already created. For our example, these are the structures HEAD and CONTACT. Now we assign the source structure HEAD to the target structures BGR00, BKN00, BKNA1, and BKNB1, and the source structure CONTACT to the target structure BKNVK. The result is shown in Figure 3.17. As you can see here, we did not assign a source structure to every target structure. For our example therefore, only a small number of possible customer master fields are transferred.

DATA MIGRATION

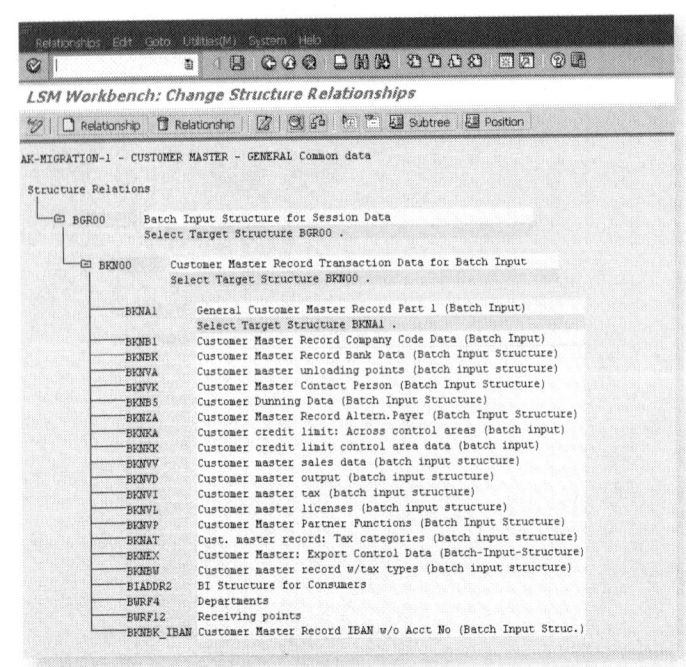

Figure 3.16: Structure relationships 1

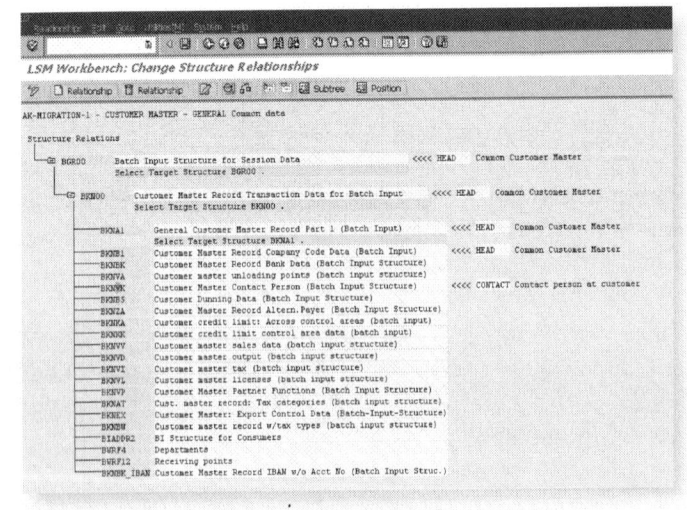

Figure 3.17: Structure relationships 2

40

As you will already know from other SAP applications, you can use CHECK (🔁) here to exclude any possible sources of error at an early stage. After checking the structure relationships, if there is an error, a corresponding message is displayed; if there are no errors, the message "There are no errors in the structure relations" appears. I recommend that, as available in this case, you always use the option for detecting errors at an early stage and perform the checks.

If you have to change a structure relationship, you must first delete the existing relationship via DELETE RELATIONSHIP (🗑 Relationship) and then create a new relationship as explained above.

If you want to know which fields belong to an SAP structure, there are two ways of finding out this information. Either click the name of the SAP structure and navigate directly to the *Data Dictionary*, or place the cursor on the code for the structure and click 🔍 . The fields are now displayed, as shown in the example structure BKNVK in Figure 3.18. Choose ⬅ to return to the STRUCTURE RELATIONSHIPS screen.

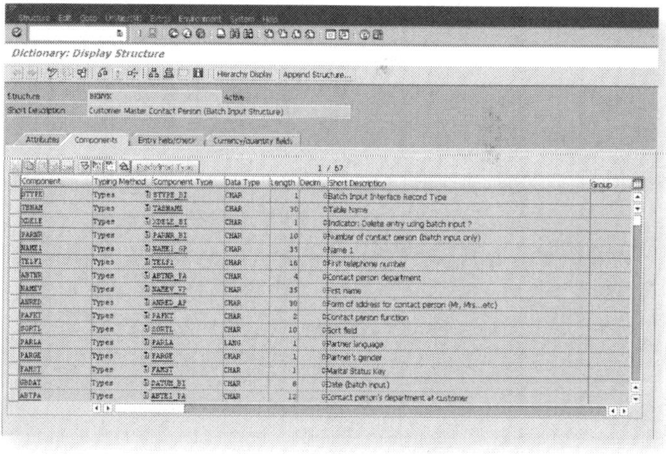

Figure 3.18: Displaying target structures

> **Control Record**
>
> Many batch input and direct input programs use a control record with the name BGR00 or BI000. Always assign the source structure of the uppermost hierarchy level ("header structure") to this record.

3.8 Maintaining Field Mapping and Conversion Rules

Now that we have defined the structures and fields and maintained the relationships of the structures to one another, in this process step we create a mapping at field level and, where necessary, assign a corresponding set of rules.

Specifically, the task in this process step is to assign corresponding source fields to the SAP target fields and to define which conversion rules are necessary for this. This process step is generally the most time-consuming, as we are working at field level.

Again we start from the LSMW main menu (see Figure 3.4) and by double-clicking MAINTAIN FIELD MAPPING AND CONVERSION RULES, obtain an overview in the form of a hierarchical tree structure with all target structures selected in Section 3.5 and the related fields (see Figure 3.19).

DATA MIGRATION

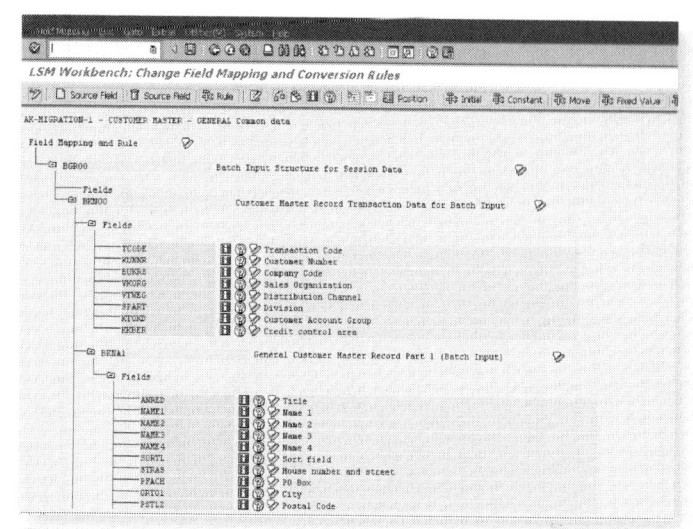

Figure 3.19: Initial field mapping

We now assign the source fields to the target fields shown. A good and easy way of obtaining this information is to request a tabular overview of the field relationships from the specialist department concerned (on paper or, preferably, in Excel). Even though this specialist department remains responsible for the data and its assignment, the IT department should be available as a contact partner for technical support.

For our example we will implement the rules shown in Table 3.1:

strucure	target field	target field name	soure field	transfer
BKN00	TCODE	transaction code	---	constant XD01
BKN00	KUNNR	customer number	HEAD-Debitor	prefix AK
BKN00	BUKRS	company code	---	value 1000
BKN00	KTOKD	costomer account group	---	constant KUNA
BKNA1	NAME1	name 1	HEAD-Name	transfer (MOVE)
BKNA1	SORTL	sort field	HEAD-Name	transfer (MOVE) shorter
BKNA1	STRAS	house number and street	HEAD-Street	transfer (MOVE)
BKNA1	ORT01	city	HEAD-Place	transfer (MOVE)
BKNA1	PSTLZ	postal code	HEAD-P_Code	transfer (MOVE)
BKNA1	LAND1	country key	HEAD-Country	conversion
BKNB1	AKONT	reconciliation account	KONTO-Akont	
BKNVK	NAME1	name 1	CONTACT-L_Name	transfer (MOVE)
BKNVK	TELF1	firs t telephone number	CONTACT-Phone	transfer (MOVE)
BKNVK	ABTNR	contact person department	CONTACT-Department	conversion
BKNVK	NAMEV	first name	CONTACT-F_Name	transfer (MOVE)
BKNVK	ANRED	form of address (Mr, Mrs...etc)	CONTACT-Titel	transfer (MOVE)
BKNVK	PAFKT	contact person function	CONTACT-Role	conversion

Table 3.1: Conversion rules

Listing these rules completes a large part of the work. The task now is to portray the field mapping in LSMW. To do this, position the cursor on the relevant target fields one after the other to assign the source field and create the required transfer rule.

In our example we begin with the field TRANSACTION CODE (TCODE). There is no source field for this target field (see Table 3.1); the default entry to be assigned is XD01. How can we implement this?

I will first explain the functions available in this LSMW menu (see Figure 3.20). Place the cursor on the corresponding code for the target field and select one of the functions explained below.

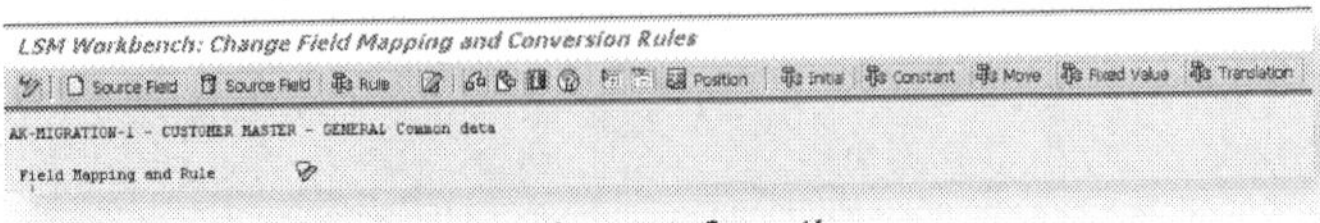

Figure 3.20: Field mapping — functions

▶ Use ✐ to switch back and forth between display and change mode (this function will be familiar to you from other menus).

▶ The function ASSIGN SOURCE FIELD Source Field allows you to assign one or more source fields. We will look at this more closely later on using the customer number (KUNNR) target field.

▶ You can use DELETE SOURCE FIELD Source Field to delete a source field assignment. If more than one source field has been assigned, a selection list appears and you can remove the field to be deleted by double-clicking it.

▶ Select INSERT RULES Rule to assign the transfer rules which you can select from the submenu that opens (see Figure 3.21).
You can also select some of the rules via the functions shown in Figure 3.20:

 Initial   Constant   Move   Fixed Value   Translation

The individual rules are explained in detail at the end of the explanation of the functions.

▶ You can insert and manage documentation using ✐ or ✐ . You can enter explanations at field or structure level.

▶ A SYNTAX CHECK is always recommended and you can start it by selecting 🔒 .

▶ You can set the DISPLAY VARIANT by selecting 🔖 . You will have noticed that in Table 3.1 and in Figure 3.19, no single field of the structure BGR00 is listed. This is because all fields of the control structure BGR00 are seen as technical fields in LSMW and default values are assigned automatically. If you are also interested in these assignments, under DETERMINE LAYOUT, activate the TECHNICAL

45

FIELDS function. All of the target fields filled with default values by the system are displayed. Values are assigned to these fields using the DEFAULT rule type (`Rule :   Default Settings`) and the fields should not be changed. However, if you change the default assignment of a field by mistake, you can reset it to the original status using EXTRAS • RESTORE DEFAULT.

Similarly to displaying and hiding technical fields, here you can set that only those fields for which code has been executed are to be visible. I have used this function in Figure 3.23 and Figure 3.24.

▶ For brief documentation on the target field on which the cursor is positioned, use the FIELD DOCUMENTATION function (🛈). For some fields, such as COMPANY CODE (BUKRS), there is also a link to more extensive documentation.

▶ You can access a selection list of the possible values available in the system via ⓘ . Whether or not a selection list is available and how the selection is formatted depends on the definition of the field in the Data Dictionary.

▶ Via EXPAND/COLLAPSE SUBTREE (🗐 🗐), you can expand or collapse the structure on which the cursor is positioned.

▶ For positioning on the line in which the cursor is located, use the POSITION (`🗐 Position`) function.

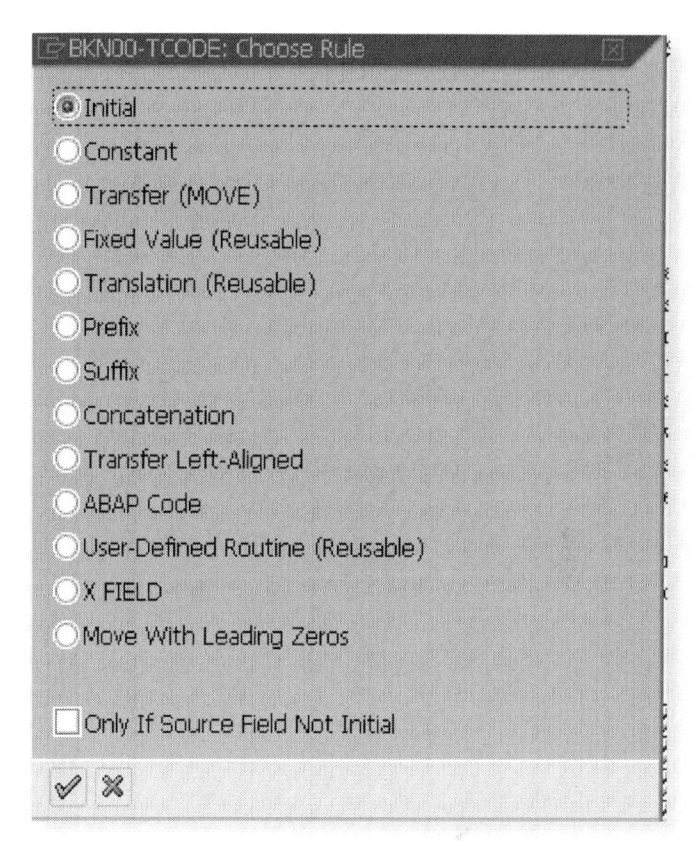

Figure 3.21: Field mapping — rules

Now we assign a default value to our first field TCODE: we assign the constant XD01.

To do this, position the cursor on the target field BKN00-TCODE and click R‍ULE (see Figure 3.20). The C‍HOOSE R‍ULE window shown in Figure 3.21 opens. Select the rule C‍ONSTANT, enter the value XD01 in the dialog box that opens, and confirm the entry with ✓.

You have assigned the first field!

Before we assign the remaining fields, I will explain the field mapping rules shown in Figure 3.21 in more detail:

- INITIAL: you can use this rule to cancel or initialize a field mapping. This deletes the entire code previously assigned to the target field and assigns an initial value that is dependent on the object type and the selected import technology to the field. With standard batch/direct input, NODATA (symbol for "no data") is entered in the field. You define the value for this in the control record (BGR00, BI000) and in our example (see Figure 3.22), the system assigned the default value "/":

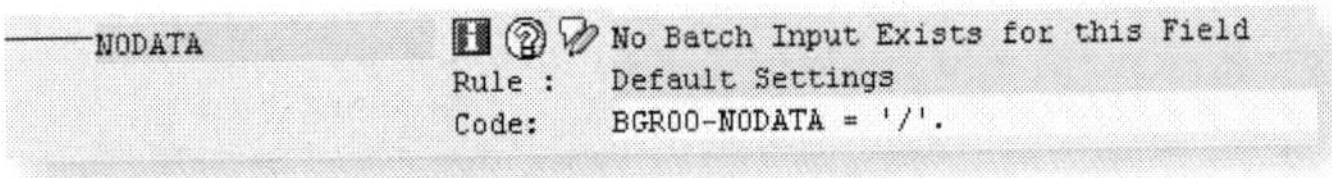

```
──NODATA            No Batch Input Exists for this Field
              Rule :  Default Settings
              Code:   BGR00-NODATA = '/'.
```

Figure 3.22: Field mapping — NODATA

For a batch input recording, "/" is entered in the target field. With BAPIs and IDocs, the ABAP command CLEAR is applied to the field. This has the effect that character fields are filled with spaces and numerical fields are filled with zeros.

- CONSTANT: this rule assigns a fixed value to the target field (see the default assignment for our first field TCODE).

- TRANSFER (MOVE): using the ABAP command MOVE, this rule transfers the data from the source field to the target field. The following transfer rules are applied dependent on the field type:

    1. 1:1 transfer for type "C" (character) and "N" (numerical).

    2. Unpack from packed fields into target fields using the ABAP instruction WRITE... TO...

Date field: if the target field has at least ten characters, the output format is according to the settings for the user master record. Otherwise, the date value is left in the internal format.

Amount field: for batch input/direct input, the amount value is formatted in accordance with the settings for the user master record. For BAPIs and IDocs, the amount value is left in the internal computing format.

The general rules valid for this ABAP command also apply in LSMW. For more extensive information, see the corresponding SAP documentation.

▶ FIXED VALUE (REUSABLE): this rule assigns a *fixed value object* (FV_fixedvalue) to the target field. This is usually a variable whose name begins with "FV_." A concrete value is assigned in the process step MAINTAIN FIXED VALUES, TRANSLATIONS, USER-DEFINED ROUTINES. In our example, we assign the field COMPANY CODE a fixed value that we can then reuse in other objects even though we only define it at a central location.

▶ TRANSLATION (REUSABLE): this rule performs a 1:1 translation according to the translation table. In the process step MAINTAIN FIXED VALUES, TRANSLATIONS, USER-DEFINED ROUTINES, you can define the values for the translation table. In our example, we implement the fields COUNTRY, DEPARTMENT, and CONTACT PARTNER FUNCTION accordingly.

▶ PREFIX: determines an arbitrary prefix that is prepended to the converted data. We will apply this when converting the field CUSTOMER NUMBER BKN00-KUNNR.

▶ SUFFIX: determines an arbitrary suffix with which the content of the source field should end.

- CONCATENATION: merges two or more source fields after the data conversion and transfers them together to the target field.

- TRANSFER LEFT-ALIGNED: transfers the content of the source field to the target field left-aligned.

- ABAP CODE: branches to the ABAP Editor, where you can edit the generated code or define your own code. The majority of the functions of the SAP standard editor are available here. You can also use the following additional functions under INSERT:

    1. Source fields: All available source fields are displayed.

    2. Global variables → see Section 8.2

    3. Global functions → see Section 8.2

- USER-DEFINED ROUTINE (REUSABLE): creates a user-defined routine (ABAP subroutine) with the name prefix "UR_" in the set of rules. In contrast to ABAP code, the routine can also be used in other objects of the project. You create this ABAP routine in the process step "Maintain Fixed Values, Translations, User-Defined Routines" (see Section 3.7).

- X FIELD: a special function for processing IDocs.

- MOVE WITH LEADING ZEROS: transfers the content of the source field to the target field with leading zeros.

- ONLY IF SOURCE FIELD NOT INITIAL: this rule should only be executed if the source field does not have the value "initial".

Now that we have learned about all of the conversion rules, we can complete the field mapping according to Table 3.1 for all source and target fields. Table 3.2 summarizes what you have to do precisely for each field and what steps are required:

Target field	Create field mapping and conversion rules
BKN00-TCODE	Place the cursor on the field BKN00-TCODE (see Figure 3.19). Click Rule. In the dialog box (see Figure 3.21), select Constant and confirm with OK. In the new input window, enter transaction code XD01 and confirm the entry.
BKN00-KUNNR	Place the cursor on the field BKN00-KUNNR (see Figure 3.19). Click the Assign Source Field button. From the list of source fields offered, select DEBITOR by double-clicking it. Click Rule. In the dialog box (see Figure 3.21), select Prefix and confirm with OK. In the new input window, enter the prefix AK and confirm the entry.

BKN00-BUKRS	Place the cursor on the field BKN00-BUKRS (see Figure 3.19). Click Rule. In the dialog box (see Figure 3.21), select Fixed Value (Reusable) and confirm with OK. In the new input window, LSMW proposes the name BUKRS — accept the name and confirm with Enter. In the subsequent dialog box, you can enter the concrete value — define 1000 here.
BKN00-KTOKD	Place the cursor on the field BKN00-KTOKD (see Figure 3.19). Click Rule. In the dialog box (see Figure 3.21), select Constant and confirm with OK. In the new input window, enter transaction code KUNA and confirm the entry.
BKNA1-NAME1	Place the cursor on the field BKNA1-NAME1 (see Figure 3.19). Click the Assign Source Field button. From the list of source fields offered, select HEAD-NAME by double-clicking it.

BKNA1-SORTL	Place the cursor on the field BKNA1-SORTL (see Figure 3.19). Click the ASSIGN SOURCE FIELD button. From the list of source fields offered, select HEAD-NAME by double-clicking it. The following message appears: "Caution: The source field is longer than the target field." This means that on transfer, the content of the source field will be shortened.
BKNA1-STRAS	Place the cursor on the field BKNA1-STRAS (see Figure 3.19). Click the ASSIGN SOURCE FIELD button. From the list of source fields offered, select HEAD-STREET by double-clicking it.
BKNA1-ORT01	Place the cursor on the field BKNA1-ORT01 (see Figure 3.19). Click the ASSIGN SOURCE FIELD button. From the list of source fields offered, select HEAD-PLACE by double-clicking it.
BKNA1-PSTLZ	Place the cursor on the field BKNA1-PSTLZ (see Figure 3.19). Click the ASSIGN SOURCE FIELD button. From the list of source fields offered, select HEAD-P_CODE by double-clicking it.

BKNA1-LAND1	Place the cursor on the field BKNA1-LAND1 (see Figure 3.19). Click the ASSIGN SOURCE FIELD button. From the list of source fields offered, select HEAD-COUNTRY by double-clicking it. Click RULE. In the dialog box (see Figure 3.21), select TRANSLATION (REUSABLE) and confirm with OK. Accept the name LAND1 suggested by LSMW and confirm.
BKNB1-AKONT	Place the cursor on the field BKNB1-AKONT (see Figure 3.19). Click RULE. In the dialog box (see Figure 3.21), select CONSTANT and confirm with OK. In the new input window, enter the value 140000 and confirm the entry.
BKNVK-NAME1	Analog to BKN00-NAME1 (transfer via MOVE).
BKNVK-TELF1	Analog to BKN00-NAME1 (transfer via MOVE).
BKNVK-ABTNR	Analog to BKNA1-LAND1 (translation).
BKNVK-NAMEV	Analog to BKN00-NAME1 (transfer via MOVE).

BKNVK-ANRED	Analog to BKN00-NAME1 (transfer via MOVE).
BKNVK-PAFKT	Analog to BKNA1-LAND1 (translation).

Table 3.2: Field mapping and conversion rules

Figure 3.23 and Figure 3.24 show the results of our field mapping in LSMW. As I have hidden the initial fields via DISPLAY VARIANT ( ), here only those fields for which mapping was defined are displayed.

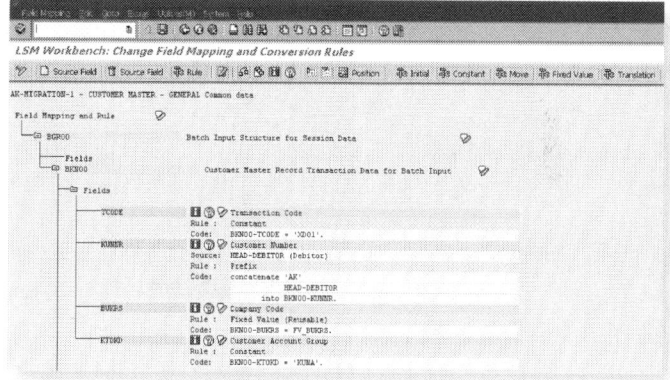

Figure 3.23: Final field mapping part 1

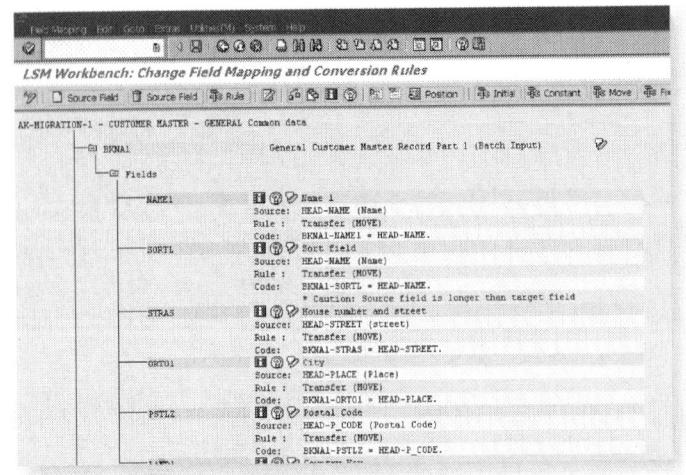

Figure 3.24: Final field mapping part 2

Before we finally end this time-consuming process step, we should instruct the LSM Workbench, using CHECK SYNTAX ( ), to generate the data conversion program and check that the syntax is correct. The message "Conversion program generated successfully" provides assurance that there are no syntax errors.

3.7 Maintaining Fixed Values, Translations, and User-Defined Routines

In this section, you define the reusable conversion rules for processing the project data.

The following rules were used for our example:

▶ Reusable fixed value for company code BKN00-BUKRS = FV_BUKRS.

▶ Reusable translation for the fields HEAD-COUNTRY, CONTACT-DEPARTMENT, and CONTACT-ROLE.

When you call up the process step MAINTAIN FIXED VALUES, TRANSLATIONS, USER-DEFINED ROUTINES, the following information is displayed for our example (see Figure 3.25):

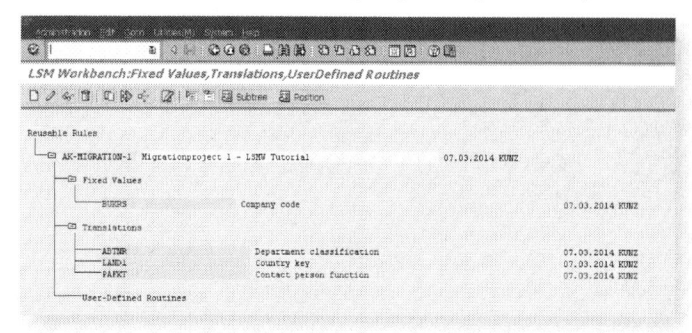

Figure 3.25: Reusable rules

Firstly we **maintain fixed values**. By double-clicking the field BUKRS (Company Code), we access the screen shown in Figure 3.26:

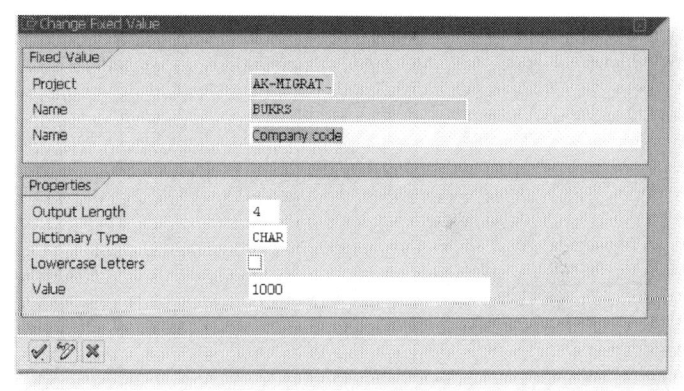

Figure 3.26: Maintaining fixed values

Here you define all of the properties of the fixed value, that is, OUTPUT LENGTH, DICTIONARY TYPE, indicator for LOWER CASE LETTERS, and the VALUE.

In the process step MAINTAIN FIELD MAPPING AND CONVERSION RULES, we entered the value 1000 for the company code (see *Table 3.2: Field mapping and conversion rules*) and therefore we do not have to make any further changes at this point.

> **Checking and Selecting Entries**
>
> Via the F4 INPUT HELP (📋), you can display and select the available entries at any time. This excludes any possible source of error.

I will explain the option of **translating** values using our example for the field COUNTRY. The file with the legacy data contains three-digit country codes. For example, USA for America, GER for Germany, and AUS for Austria. In the SAP system however, the following designations have been created: US, DE, AU. Therefore, we have to translate the legacy data using the appropriate translation rules:

AUS → AU

GER → DE

USA → US

You create a reusable rule for the translation in multiple steps (see Figure 3.27 to 3.29): double-clicking the translation LAND1 in Figure 3.25 takes you to the first step for translation maintenance (see Figure 3.27):

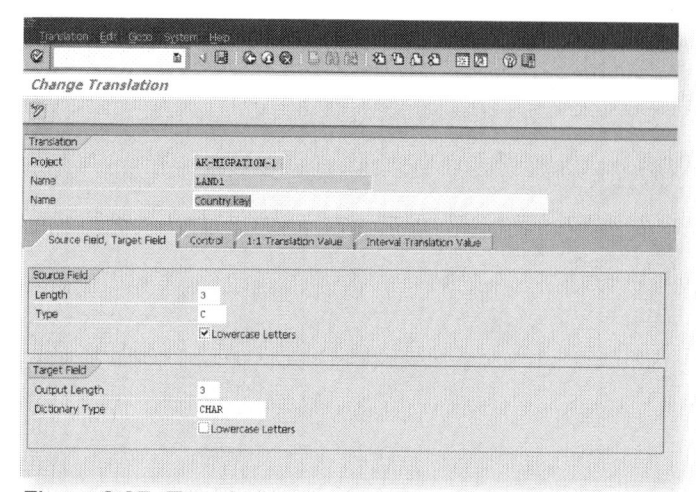

Figure 3.27: Translation 1

SOURCE FIELD, TARGET FIELD: here we can accept the values proposed by the LSM Workbench for the source and target fields and move on to the next tab.

CONTROL: on this screen, we define which type of translation should be used and which alternatives should be applied successively. For our example we choose 1:1 translation and leave the field INITIAL VALUE selected if no entry should be found in the translation table (see Figure 3.28).

DATA MIGRATION

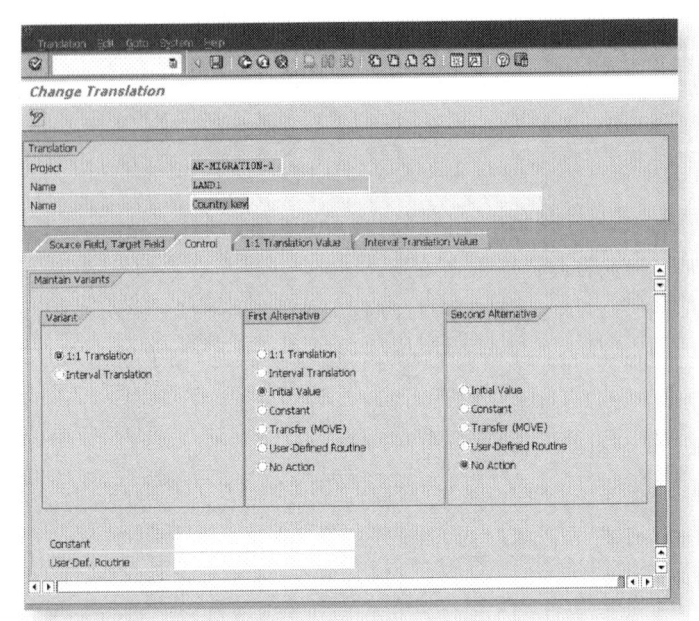

Figure 3.28: Translation 2

1:1 TRANSLATION VALUE: on the third tab, enter the value of the source field under OLD VALUE and the value of the target field under NEW VALUE (see Figure 3.29). Again, note that input help (F4) is available for the field NEW VALUE and should be used. Note also that only those translations for which the OK indicator is set are considered. Therefore, in our example, GBR and ESP would not be converted.

In addition to manual entry in the table itself, you can also import the values from a file using the UPLOAD function ( ). The data should then be available as text file (separated by tab stops).

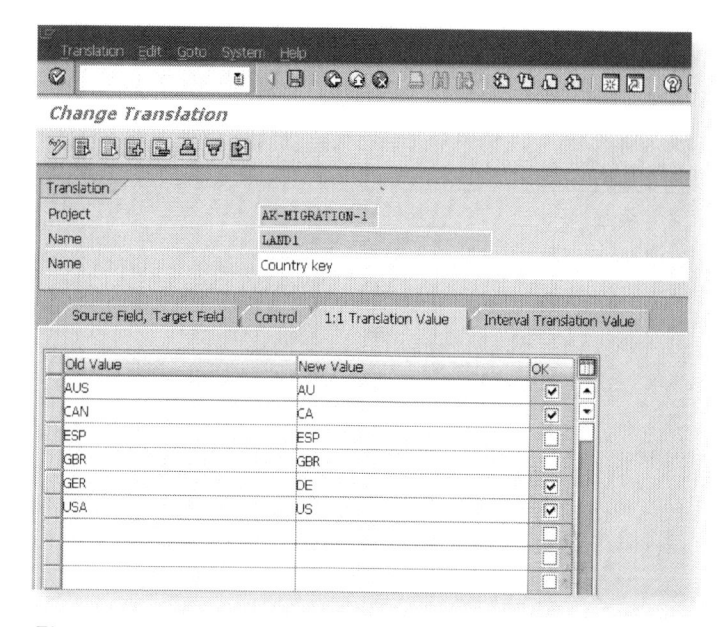

Figure 3.29: Translation 3

A great advantage is that the translation can be used as an automatic value collector for the conversion. After execution of the process step CONVERT DATA, all values for which there is no translation are entered in the translation table: the new value corresponds to the old value and the OK field is not set (see Figure 3.29). Therefore, you only have to set the target values (preferably using the input help) such that they are accepted by SAP, and then set the OK indicator.

You activate the automatic value collector by clicking the CONTROL tab (see Figure 3.28), scrolling to the bottom, and under MISCELLANEOUS, activating the field 1:1 TRANSLATION TABLE ADDED TO AUTOMATICALLY (see Figure 3.30).

Figure 3.30: Translation 4

On the INTERVAL TRANSLATION VALUE tab, you can specify entire intervals for translation to a value. You can also enter this information directly or import it from a file via UPLOAD.

The third option in this process step is the creation of **user-defined routines**. ABAP code, which you can add to any target field in the process step "Maintain Field Mapping and Conversion Rules," is valid exclusively for this one LSMW and thus cannot be used in other LSMWs. However, if you want to use the code at multiple points within a project, you can create user-defined routines to do this. The prerequisite for this is that in the previous process step, you have already assigned the rule USER-DEFINED ROUTINE (REUSABLE) to the corresponding target field. In this case, you can now create your own rule that you use within the project in various subprojects.

3.8 Specifying Files

You create the *data conversion file* from the data to be migrated. To do this, you must first describe all files intended for data migration via the process step SPECIFY FILES. Double-click this process step in the LSMW main menu (see Figure 3.4) to navigate to the following input screen:

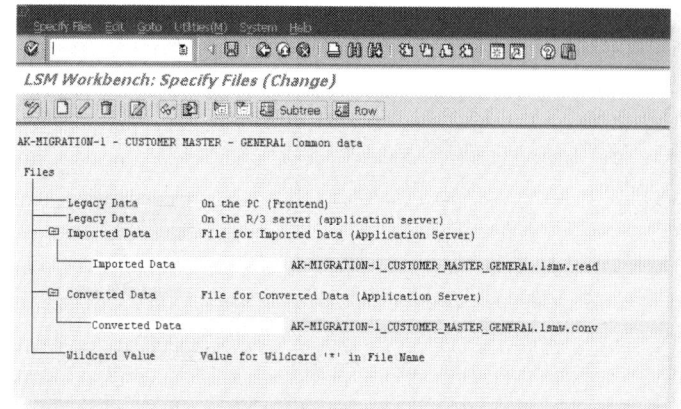

Figure 3.31: Specifying files 1

Here you specify the following files:

1. File(s) on the PC and/or SAP server
2. File for the imported data
3. File for the converted data

As you can see in Figure 3.31, the system already makes proposals for the imported and **converted data**. The file name is composed from the codes for the project, subproject, and object of the current LSMW (separated by underscores): AK-MIGRATION-1_CUSTOMER_MASTER_GENERAL. The file extensions are LSMW.READ for the file of the imported data and LSMW.CON for the file of the converted data. I generally recommend that you accept this proposal. However, in our example, you will receive an error message, as the complete file name for the converted data can be a maximum of 45 characters and the generated name exceeds this condition by one character. Double-click the name of the converted file to navigate to MAINTAIN FILE NAME and then change the name. This results in the following name:

63

► Imported data:

AK-MIGRATION-1_CUSTOMER_MASTER_GE-NERAL.LSMW.READ

► Converted data:

AK-MIGRATION-1_CUSTOMER_MASTER_ALL.LSMW.CONV

Now we have to specify the files for the legacy data, that is, the data to be imported. You can import the legacy data from the frontend PC or from the SAP application server. In our example, the data is available as two Excel files (see Figure 3.1 and Figure 3.2). Therefore, we use the import from PC option.

Before the data can be imported, the Excel files must first be converted into TXT files, that is, into the format TEXT (SEPARATED BY TAB STOP).

For our two example files, this results in the following names:

► Contact.txt
► Header.txt

I will briefly demonstrate how we assign these files in LSMW. To do this, in the process step SPECIFY FILES, we position the cursor on the line LEGACY DATA — ON THE PC (FRONTEND) (see Figure 3.31) and select ADD ENTRY (). In the dialog box that opens (see Figure 3.32), enter the file name and path. The best way to do this is to use the input help available.

Furthermore, you must maintain the data properties of the five items of data shown in Figure 3.32 (DEBITOR HEADER DATA).

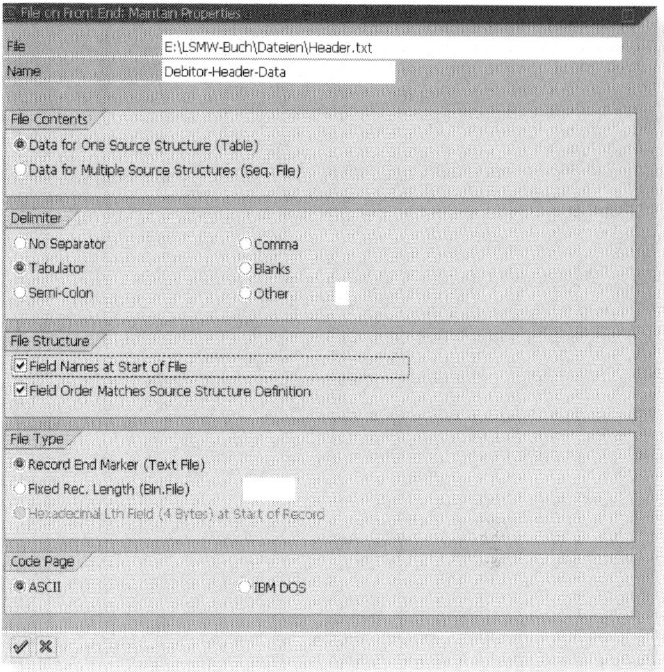

Figure 3.32: File properties

▶ FILE CONTENTS

Here, we select DATA FOR ONE SOURCE STRUCTURE (TABLE), as the content of our files is available in table form, all records have the same record structure, and all belong to the same source structure.

If a file contains records for various source structures, you have to use the order to define which records belong together. In this case, select DATA FOR MULTIPLE SOURCE STRUCTURES (SEQ. FILE).

▶ DELIMITER

I recommend that you use the tab character as delimiter/separator. Semi-colons, commas, and blanks can easily occur within a text field and can cause undesired field shifts as a consequence. For our example we therefore choose TABULATOR.

▶ FILE STRUCTURE

As we leave the field headings as the first line to provide a better overview in our TXT file, here we have to select the field FIELD NAMES AT START OF FILE. If we use the field names at the start for table-type files, the order of the fields within the file does not have to match the order of the source fields within the source structure. In this case we would deselect the option FIELD ORDER MATCHES SOURCE STRUCTURE DEFINITION. However, in our example the two orders match and so we select the corresponding option.

▶ FILE TYPE

Here we select RECORD END MARKER (TEXT FILE). You can always use this if the data was exported from Excel. As this is the option most frequently used, LSMW proposes this file type.

FIXED RECORD LENGTH (BINARY FILE) means that the legacy data is available in files in which each record is the same length. An example application would be files provided by a mainframe computer.

HEXADECIMAL LENGTH FIELD (4 BYTES) AT START OF RECORD was used in the migration from R/2 to R/3 and is rarely used today.

▶ CODE PAGE

For our example we use ASCII code. If the data in the legacy system has been coded with a different character set, LSMW can convert this. The prerequisite is that the character set in which the legacy data is available was specified.

All settings detailed above must be configured accordingly for the item data (customer) as well. This produces the following result (see Figure 3.33):

```
AK-MIGRATION-1 - CUSTOMER MASTER - GENERAL Common data
Files
   Legacy Data           On the PC (Frontend)
      Debitor-Contact-Data    E:\LSMW-Buch\Dateien\Contact.txt
                              Data for One Source Structure (Table)
                              Separator Tabulator
                              Field Names at Start of File
                              Field Order Matches Source Structure Definition
                              With Record End Indicator (Text File)
                              Code Page ASCII
      Debitor-Header-Data     E:\LSMW-Buch\Dateien\Header.txt
                              Data for One Source Structure (Table)
                              Separator Tabulator
                              Field Names at Start of File
                              Field Order Matches Source Structure Definition
                              With Record End Indicator (Text File)
                              Code Page ASCII
   Legacy Data           On the R/3 server (application server)
   Imported Data         File for Imported Data (Application Server)
      Imported Data           AK-MIGRATION-1_CUSTOMER_MASTER_GENERAL.lsmw.read
   Converted Data        File for Converted Data (Application Server)
      Converted Data          AK-MIGRATION-1_CUSTOMER_MASTER.lsmw.conv
   Wildcard Value        Value for Wildcard '*' in File Name
```

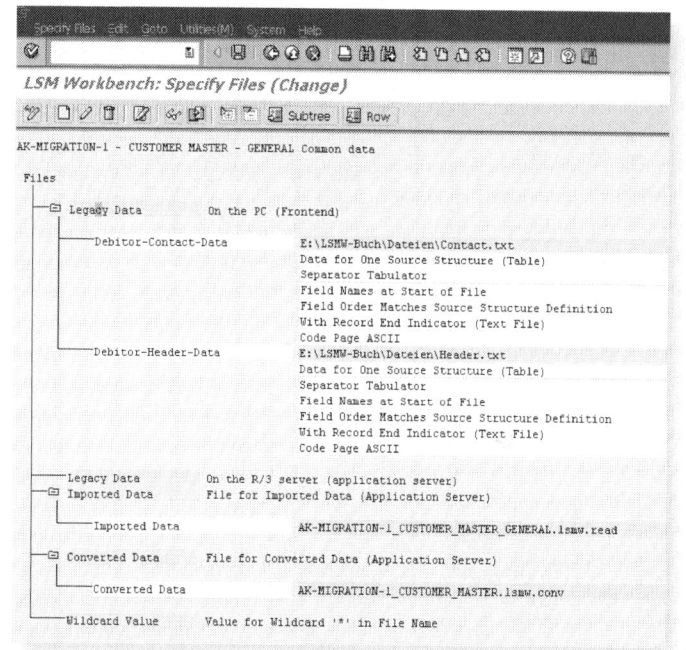

Figure 3.33: Specifying files 2

Attentive readers will have noted that there is a further configuration option in Figure 3.33: WILDCARD VALUE. You can use this option if the source data has been stored in multiple sets of files whose names only have a few different characters.

> **SAP Home Directory**
>
> LSMW uses the *SAP HOME DIRECTORY* of the SAP application server as file path. You can use transaction AL11 to display all SAP directories.

The files used in our project are defined under the directory DIR_HOME (see Figure 3.34). You will also find the physical path of the SAP Home Directory there.

Figure 3.34: SAP Directory

3.9 Assigning Files

We now assign the files defined in Section 3.8 to the source structures. To do this, from the LSMW main menu (see Figure 3.4), call up the process step ASSIGN FILES. Place the cursor on the source structure HEAD and select ASSIGN FILE (Assignment). The files already defined are listed. In our example, we assign the debitor header data to the source structure HEAD and the debitor contact data to the source structure CONTACT. The result is shown in Figure 3.35.

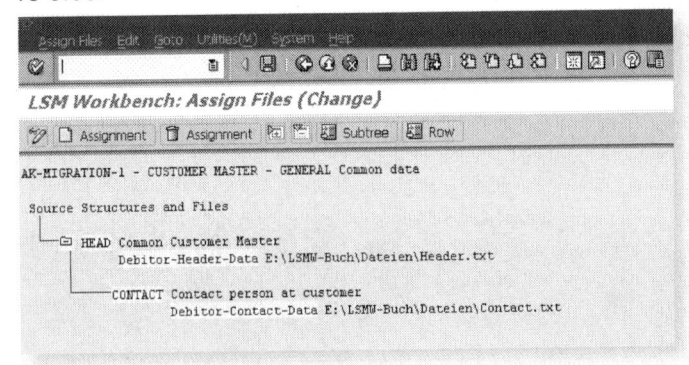

Figure 3.35: Assigning files

The settings are saved and we proceed to the next step, importing the files.

3.10 Importing Files

We also call up the process step READ DATA from the LSMW main menu (see Figure 3.4). The system first checks whether the data import program is still up-to-date. If not, it is automatically regenerated. Then the screen shown in Figure 3.36 appears. There you can decide whether you want to import all legacy data or only a subset of the legacy data. To do this, you can restrict the quantity of data to be imported in the GENERAL SELECTION PARAMETERS section. This is very helpful for initial test purposes for a new LSMW project. However, for live migration, you should always select all data to ensure processing without any gaps.

If, when defining the source fields, you marked one or more source fields as selection parameters, these fields are offered for selection. In Section 3.4 (Maintaining Source Fields), we marked the field DEBITOR accordingly. This means that it is now offered for selection and we can thus select a specific customer for test purposes.

You can also set the following indicators:

▶ VALUE FIELDS are implemented in computing format (with a decimal point).

▶ DATE VALUES are implemented in internal format (YYYYMMDD).

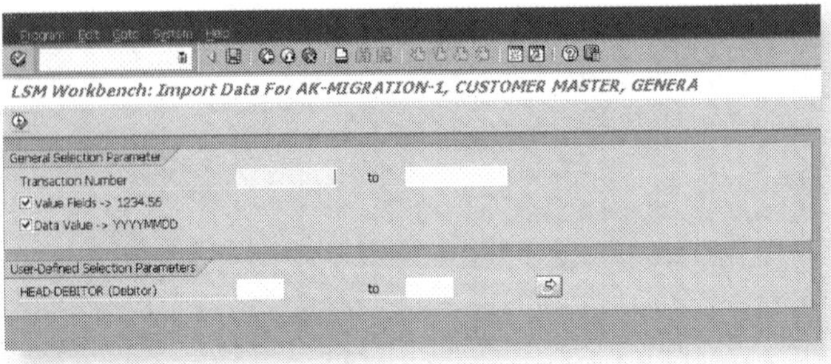

Figure 3.36: Importing data

Accept the settings shown in Figure 3.36 and click EXECUTE ( ).

Both files from the legacy system are now imported and converted into a uniform technical format.

After completion of the import operation, a log is created (see Figure 3.37). This shows whether this process step was executed successfully and all records processed. For our example, seven data records from the "Head" file and eight records from the "Contact" file were read.

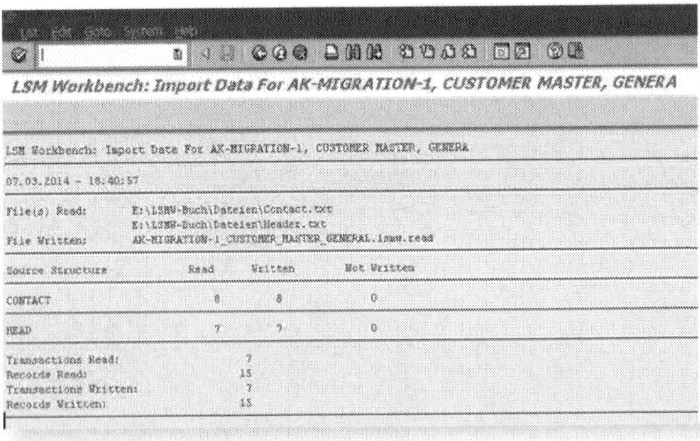

Figure 3.37: Importing data — log

> **Wildcards**
>
> If you use placeholders (*wildcards*) in the file names of the input files and you have defined at least one value for the placeholders, a selection parameter is also offered for the wildcard. If you have not entered any information here, all defined wildcard values are processed.

3.11 Displaying Imported Data

You now want to display the imported data in SAP. The following section explains how this works. In the LSMW main menu (see Figure 3.4), select DISPLAY READ DATA. You can then decide whether to display all of the data or only part of the data. For our test purposes, for which we have selected only a small data volume, it makes sense to display all of the data and thus without making a partial selection, we select CONTINUE ( ) to proceed to the list shown in Figure 3.38.

Figure 3.38: Displaying imported data 1

For the purposes of the overview, the individual record types (Head and Contact) are shown in different colors.

I will briefly show how you can display the information for a line more clearly. To do this, position the cursor on a line for which you want to evaluate the contents and click DETAILED DISPLAY (Field Contents). As shown in Figure 3.39, the data is listed clearly in a table. This enables a faster analysis and early detection of errors.

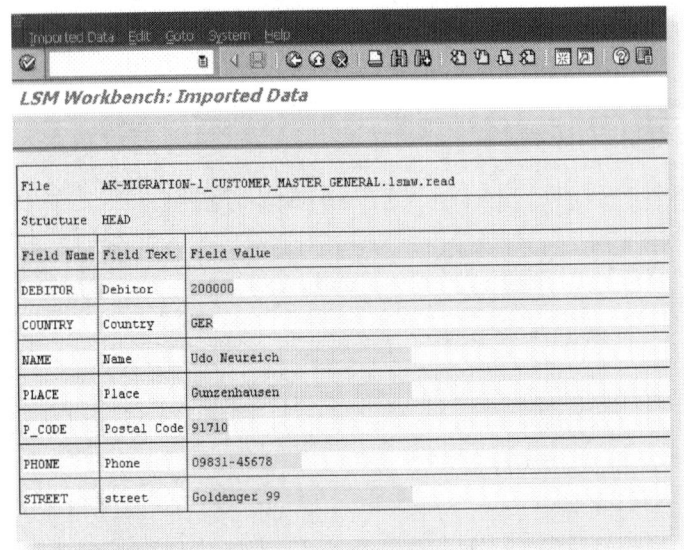

Field Name	Field Text	Field Value
DEBITOR	Debitor	200000
COUNTRY	Country	GER
NAME	Name	Udo Neureich
PLACE	Place	Gunzenhausen
P_CODE	Postal Code	91710
PHONE	Phone	09831-45678
STREET	street	Goldanger 99

File: AK-MIGRATION-1_CUSTOMER_MASTER_GENERAL.lsmw.read
Structure: HEAD

Figure 3.39: Displaying imported data 2

Another option for data preparation is the function Change Display, which you can use to switch between single-line and multiple line displays.

The colors of the individual hierarchy levels are displayed in a LEGEND (Display Colour Legend).

3.12 Converting Data

The file of *imported* data must now be transformed into the file of *converted* data. You initiate this process by selecting the process step CONVERT DATA (see Figure 3.4). Similarly to the process step READ DATA (see Figure 3.36), on the GENERAL SELECTION PARAMETERS screen, you can select the volume of data that you want to convert for test purposes.

If, when defining the source fields, you marked one or more source fields as selection parameters, these fields are offered as selection parameters here. In our example, this is the field HEAD-DEBITOR. Again, the following applies: if you use a wildcard in the file names of the input files and have defined at least one value for the wildcard, you will also receive a selection parameter for the corresponding files. If you have not entered any information here, all defined wildcard values are processed.

A log of the data conversion program (see Figure 3.40) is provided. You will recognize that in our example, the number of records read is different to the number of records written. In the subsequent process step DISPLAY CONVERTED DATA, you can look at the cause of this deviation and evaluate and analyze the converted data.

The system first checks whether the data conversion program is still up-to-date. If it is not, it is automatically regenerated.

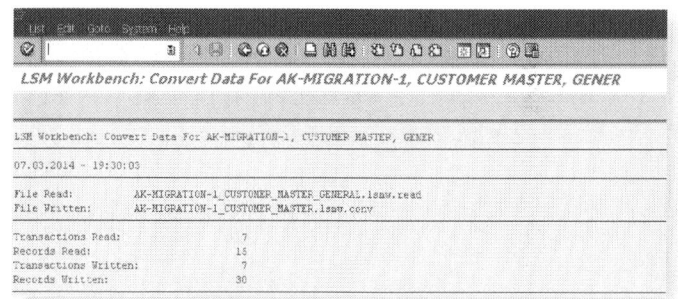

Figure 3.40: Converting data

3.13 Displaying Converted Data

We have made a lot of progress with importing and converting our example data. Now we will look at the converted data to ensure that all conversion rules have been successfully executed.

To do this, in the LSMW main menu (see Figure 3.4), proceed to the process step DISPLAY CONVERTED DATA, EXECUTE. A selection screen appears (see Figure 3.41) on which you can restrict the volume of data displayed.

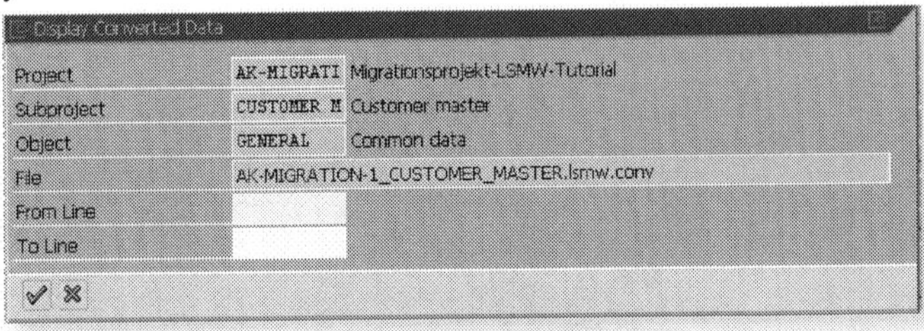

Figure 3.41: Displaying converted data 1

The only difference to the selection screen in the process step DISPLAY READ DATA (see Section 3.11) is in the file name. The converted data is stored in the following file in the SAP system:

AK-MIGRATION-1_CUSTOMER_MASTER_ALL.lsmw.conv

The imported data is stored in the following file in the SAP system:

AK-MIGRATION-1_CUSTOMER_MASTER_GENERAL.lsmw.read

As already explained in Section 3.8, the data is stored in the SAP HOME DIRECTORY (see Figure 3.34).

Figure 3.42 shows the converted data. As already mentioned in Section 3.12, the number of records deviates from that of the legacy data. This is the case in most LSMW projects and is due to the different structure of legacy data compared to the SAP format. However, the number of data units (seven customers in our example) should match.

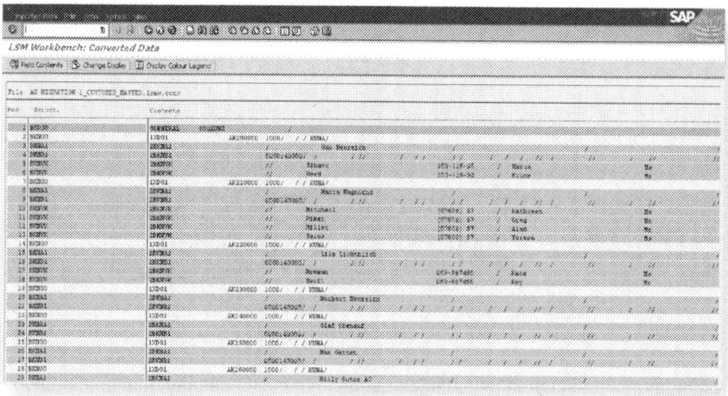

Figure 3.42: Displaying converted data 2

I will briefly show how the number of converted data records arose.

As Figure 3.42 shows, one BGR00 record is created for each conversion file. For each customer, the system creates one BKN00 record, one BKNA1 record, and one BKNB1 record, as well as one BKNVK record for each contact person. For seven customers and eight contact persons read, that makes (1+7*3+8) 30 written records (see Figure 3.40).

As described in Section 3.11, you can also choose between single-line and multiple line display, display the color legend, and by clicking on a line, obtain a detailed display of the corresponding record (see Figure 3.43).

File AK-MIGRATION-1_CUSTOMER_MASTER.lsmw.conv		
Structure BKNVK		
Fld Name	Fld Text	FldValue
STYPE	Batch Input Interface Record Type	2
TBNAM	Table Name	BKNVK
XDELE	Indicator: Delete entry using batch input ?	/
PARNR	Number of contact person (batch input only)	/
NAME1	Name 1	Singer
TELF1	First telephone number	303-126-95
ABTNR	Contact person department	0003
NAMEV	First name	Maria
ANRED	Form of address for contact person (Mr, Mrs...etc)	Ms
PAFKT	Contact person function	01
SORTL	Sort field	/
PARLA	Partner language	/

Figure 3.43: Displaying converted data 3

At this point, you can check whether the conversion of the individual fields was successful. In our example, amongst other things, a 1:1 translation should be executed on the field CONTACT PERSON DEPARTMENT. As shown in Figure 3.43, this was executed successfully (value in legacy file SALES translated to 0003). Fields that have a forward slash (/) are interpreted as "no entry" for further processing, meaning that the field content is retained.

3.14 Creating Batch Input Sessions

Now that we have completed all preparations and the data has been converted and is available, we can proceed to the next process step. What this is depends on the import technology selected in the process step MAINTAIN OBJECT

ATTRIBUTES (Section 3.2). In the example described, we selected the STANDARD BATCH INPUT import technology (see Figure 3.6). Therefore, the next process step offered in the LSMW main menu (see Figure 3.4) is CREATE BATCH INPUT SESSION. When you select this by double-clicking it, the screen shown in Figure 3.44 appears.

The system proposes the name of the file with the converted data and you should retain this name, in our example: AK-MIGRATION-1_CUSTOMER_MASTER.lsmw.conv.

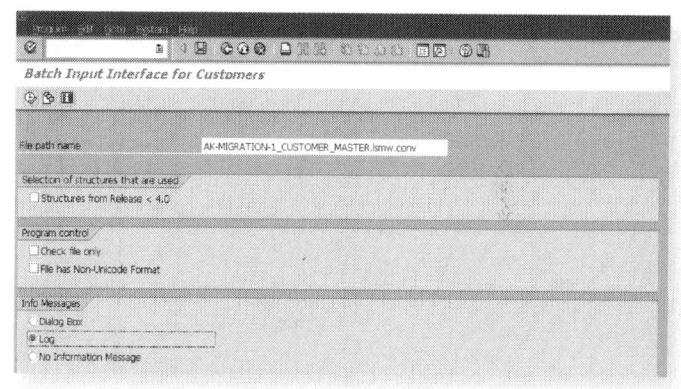

Figure 3.44: Creating batch input

The other setting options are heavily dependent on the respective batch input program.

In our case, under SELECTION OF STRUCTURES THAT ARE USED, you could select the field STRUCTURES FROM RELEASE < 4.0. You would thus inform the system that data records transferred in the file match the structures valid before Release 4.0, meaning that they were very probably transferred from a very old SAP system. From SAP Release 4.0, the lengths of the fields TRANSACTION CODE (TCODE) and TABLE NAME (TABNAME) were extended, and therefore all subsequent fields shift to the right. The old structures are therefore no longer compatible with the new structures.

If you select the parameter STRUCTURES FROM RELEASE < 4.0, the data transfer report prepares the data records delivered such that they match the new structures and can be processed. In our example, this is not necessary, as the source data is available in a current format.

> **External Interface**
>
> If you use an external interface to prepare your data for the SAP system, you will have to adapt this interface to the new structures. It is highly probable that the option of processing shorter data records will be removed in a subsequent release.

In the PROGRAM CONTROL area, you can also select CHECK FILE ONLY to check the batch input file before creating the session. The batch input session is not created and there is no processing. Errors in the file that would lead to a cancellation of processing are thus detected early and reported at an early stage.

Examples of file errors that would cause a cancellation are:

▶ Client missing in the session prefix.

▶ The header record for a transaction is missing.

▶ The table name of a data record is missing or invalid.

I have checked this for our example and received the message NO CANCELLATION SITUATIONS DETECTED.

Selecting the parameter FILE HAS NON-UNICODE-FORMAT means that the file is processed in a non-unicode format, alternatively in UTF-8 format (read or written).

In the last area, INFO MESSAGES, you can select the form in which information that occurs during processing is made available to you and whether you generally receive information messages. In our example, I decided on presentation in log form. From the information shown in Figure 3.45, we can see that a session with the name GENERAL was created. In this batch input process, the session name always corresponds to the object name from the LSM Workbench (see Figure 3.3).

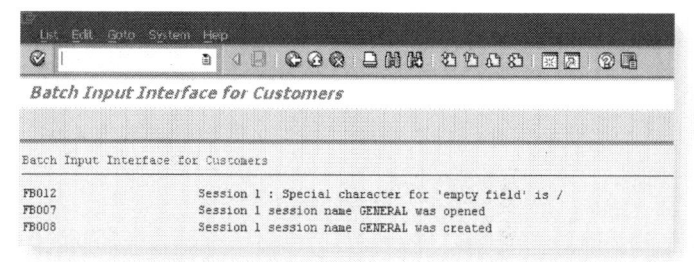

```
List Edit Goto System Help

Batch Input Interface for Customers

Batch Input Interface for Customers
FB012          Session 1 : Special character for 'empty field' is /
FB007          Session 1 session name GENERAL was opened
FB008          Session 1 session name GENERAL was created
```

Figure 3.45: Batch input log

As already mentioned, the selection screen (see Figure 3.44) is always based on the corresponding batch input program. Alternatively, the name of the batch input session could be changed at this point and the number of transactions per BTCI session determined. We will return to this topic in Section 4.2.

3.15 Processing Batch Input Sessions

Now we come to the last process step of our LSMW main menu shown in Figure 3.4. In the process step RUN BATCH INPUT SESSION, the data is written to the SAP database.

Once you have executed this process step, the system takes you to the SAP standard transaction BATCH INPUT MONITORING (SM35). Here, only those batch input sessions that belong to the selected object are displayed; in our case, all sessions with the name GENERAL (see Figure 3.46).

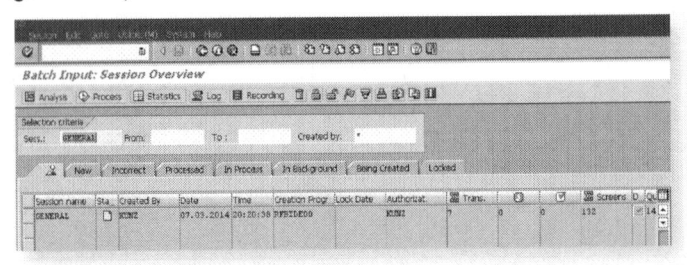

Figure 3.46: Session overview

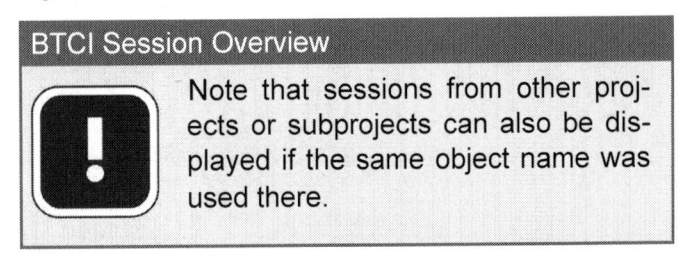

> **BTCI Session Overview**
>
> Note that sessions from other projects or subprojects can also be displayed if the same object name was used there.

Below I will explain the options available when processing the batch input session in more detail. I will also provide additional information on this topic to give inexperienced LSMW users as complete an overview as possible. For experienced consultants, the processing of the batch input session ends the example. They can skip the following detailed explanations and continue with Section 3.16.

Firstly, a brief explanation of batch input processing: in the early days of SAP, batch input was the only technology for transferring external data into the SAP system. Even though other technologies are now available (IDocs, BAPIs), the batch input method is still the most frequently used as it offers extensive user support and is very similar to dialog functions.

In the overview shown in Figure 3.46, select the session that you want to process and click PROCESS SESSION (Process). Three options are offered for processing the session (see PROCESSING MODE in Figure 3.47):

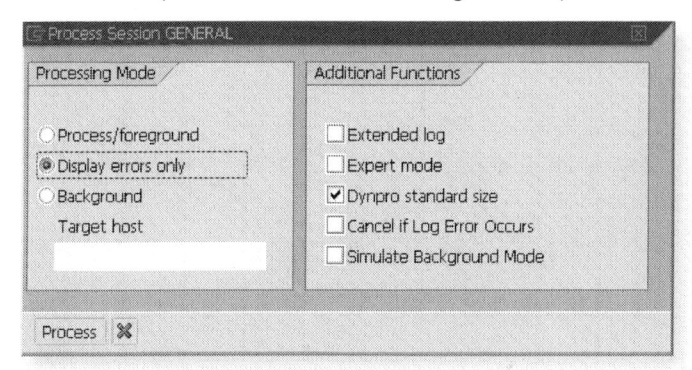

Figure 3.47: Processing batch input 1

▶ PROCESS/FOREGROUND

... means that each individual screen of the transaction is displayed with the inserted data. You can correct incorrect entries directly and proceed to the next screen with the EN-TER KEY. You can exit the current transaction and navigate to the next transaction by entering OK CODE/N. You can end the complete processing of the batch input session with OK CODE/BEND. However, you can always start it again at a later point in time. This mode is only suitable for a small number of transactions and is used mostly for test purposes.

▶ DISPLAY ERRORS ONLY

... means that the data is imported in the background until an error occurs. In this case, the system switches to dialog processing and the corresponding *dynpro* (dynamic program, also referred to as "screen") is displayed, allowing you to add missing entries or correct errors. The processing then returns to the background until the complete session has been processed or until a new error situation occurs.

81

I have used this mode for our example — in the selection window (see Figure 3.47), I selected DISPLAY ERRORS ONLY and then PROCESS. As the session was processed without any errors, the information shown in Figure 3.48 is displayed.

▶ BACKGROUND

... means that the batch input session is planned for processing in the background. Active intervention in the event of an error is not possible.

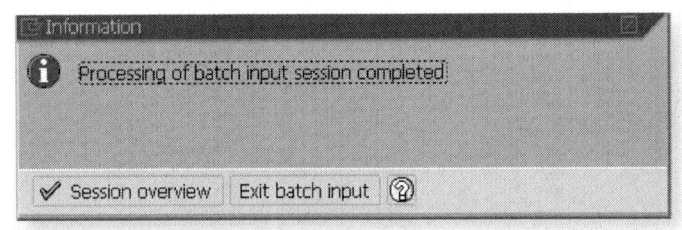

Figure 3.48: Processing batch input 2

At this point, you can end the batch input processing or return to the session overview.

Once all transactions in a batch input session have been successfully processed, the complete session is deleted. This is the case in our example. The session is no longer included in any of the possible statuses.

Alternatively, when creating the batch input session, you can specify that the session is to be *held*: in this case it cannot be processed again, but it is retained for audit and documentation purposes.

This completes the batch input topic. If you require more detailed information, see the corresponding SAP literature.

3.16 Object Overview

As announced in Section 3.1.5, at the end of the example project we now return to the OBJECT OVERVIEW function.

Switch to the LSMW main menu; now that all of the process steps have been processed, it looks as shown in Figure 3.49:

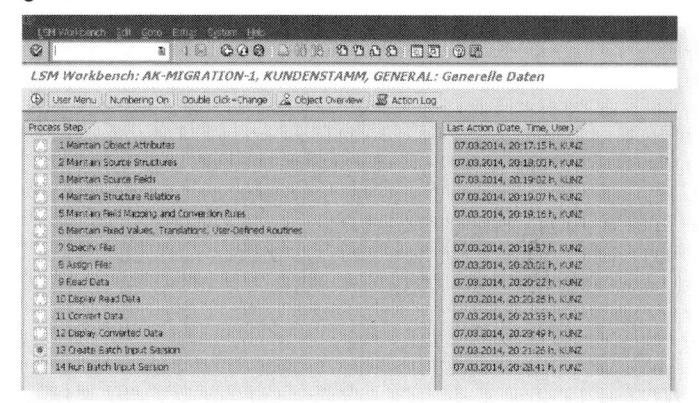

Figure 3.49: Navigation screen

Click the OBJECT OVERVIEW button and then select whether to display the information in list or table form.

This overview was still empty at the beginning of the creation of the LSMW, but now contains all definitions undertaken for the object GENERAL. Specifically, Figure 3.50 shows all object information, source structures, target structures, and structure relationships in list form.

```
LSM Workbench: Object Overview (List)
  Overview in Table Format    Overview of Reusable Rules

Legacy System Migration Workbench: Object Information

This list generated on      07.03.2014 At 20:41:26 . R/3 System    I62 .

Project:                AK-MIGRATION-1  Migrationsprojekt-LSMW-Tutorial
Subproject:             CUSTOMER MASTER Customer Master
Object:                 GENERAL         Common Data
Data Transfer Program:  RFBIDE00
Data Transfer Method:   B (Batch Input)

Source Structures

HEAD - Header Data
  CONTACT - Contact Data

Target Structures

BGR00 - Batch Input Structure for Session Data
  BKN00 - Customer Master Record Transaction Data for Batch Input
    BKNA1 - General Customer Master Record Part 1 (Batch Input)
    BKNB1 - Customer Master Record Company Code Data (Batch Input)
    BKNVK - Customer Master Contact Person (Batch Input Structure)

Structure Relations

BGR00 <=== HEAD
  BKN00 <=== HEAD
    BKNA1 <=== HEAD
    BKNB1 <=== HEAD
    BKNVK <=== CONTACT
```

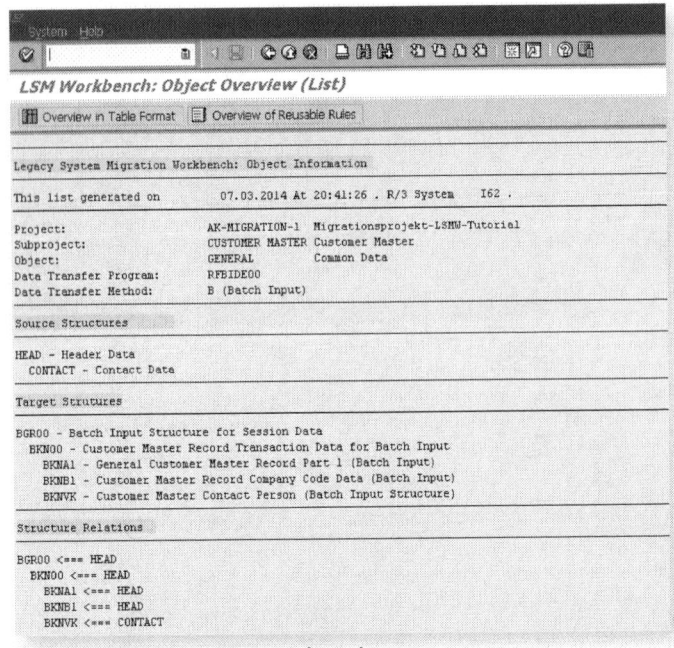

Figure 3.50: Object overview 1

It is worth scrolling down further in the display to also analyze the source and target fields (see Figure 3.51) and the field mapping (see Figure 3.52).

Although the list form appears clearer at first glance, I would still recommend displaying the information in table form to enable a better comparison with the field mapping conduct in Section 3.6.

DATA MIGRATION

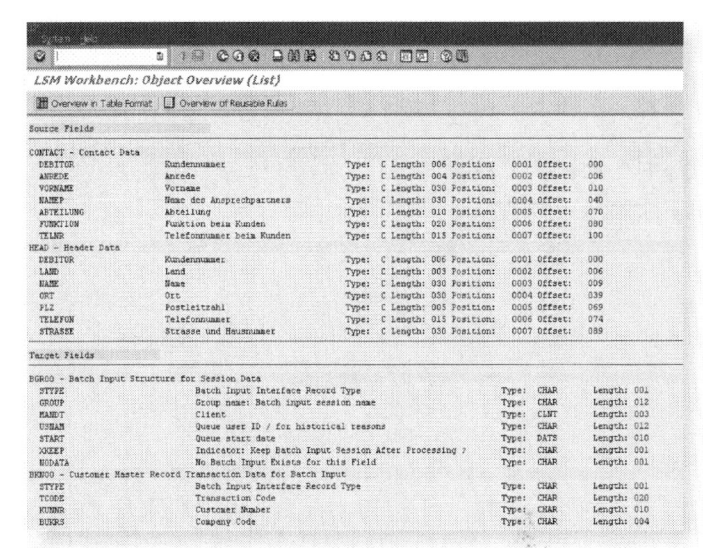

```
LSM Workbench: Object Overview (List)

Overview in Table Format    Overview of Reusable Rules

Source Fields

CONTACT - Contact Data
  DEBITOR       Kundennummer                    Type: C Length: 006 Position: 0001 Offset: 000
  ANREDE        Anrede                          Type: C Length: 004 Position: 0002 Offset: 006
  VORNAME       Vorname                         Type: C Length: 030 Position: 0003 Offset: 010
  NAMEP         Name des Ansprechpartners       Type: C Length: 030 Position: 0004 Offset: 040
  ABTEILUNG     Abteilung                       Type: C Length: 010 Position: 0005 Offset: 070
  FUNKTION      Funktion beim Kunden            Type: C Length: 020 Position: 0006 Offset: 080
  TELNR         Telefonnummer beim Kunden       Type: C Length: 015 Position: 0007 Offset: 100
HEAD - Header Data
  DEBITOR       Kundennummer                    Type: C Length: 006 Position: 0001 Offset: 000
  LAND          Land                            Type: C Length: 003 Position: 0002 Offset: 006
  NAME          Name                            Type: C Length: 030 Position: 0003 Offset: 009
  ORT           Ort                             Type: C Length: 030 Position: 0004 Offset: 039
  PLZ           Postleitzahl                    Type: C Length: 005 Position: 0005 Offset: 069
  TELEFON       Telefonnummer                   Type: C Length: 015 Position: 0006 Offset: 074
  STRASSE       Strasse und Hausnummer          Type: C Length: 030 Position: 0007 Offset: 089

Target Fields

BGR00 - Batch Input Structure for Session Data
  STYPE         Batch Input Interface Record Type                              Type: CHAR  Length: 001
  GROUP         Group name: Batch input session name                           Type: CHAR  Length: 012
  MANDT         Client                                                         Type: CLNT  Length: 003
  USNAM         Queue user ID / for historical reasons                         Type: CHAR  Length: 012
  START         Queue start date                                               Type: DATE  Length: 010
  XKEEP         Indicator: Keep Batch Input Session After Processing ?         Type: CHAR  Length: 001
  NODATA        No Batch Input Exists for this Field                           Type: CHAR  Length: 001
BKN00 - Customer Master Record Transaction Data for Batch Input
  STYPE         Batch Input Interface Record Type                              Type: CHAR  Length: 001
  TCODE         Transaction Code                                               Type: CHAR  Length: 020
  KUNNR         Customer Number                                                Type: CHAR  Length: 010
  BUKRS         Company Code                                                   Type: CHAR  Length: 004
```

Figure 3.51: Object overview 2

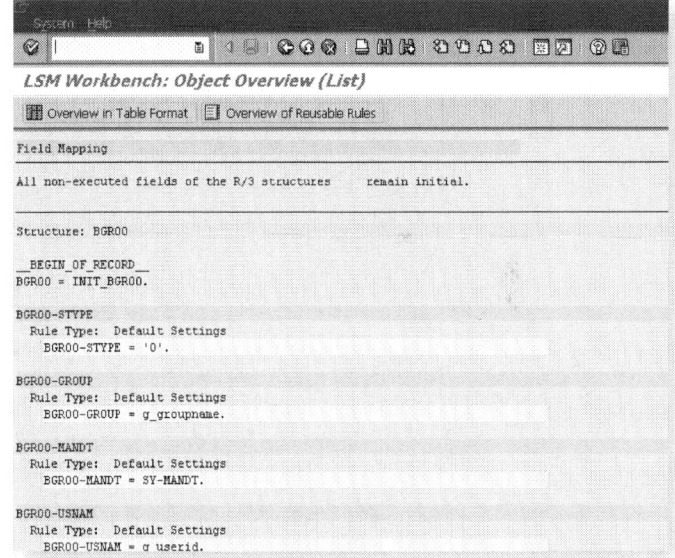

```
LSM Workbench: Object Overview (List)

Overview in Table Format    Overview of Reusable Rules

Field Mapping

All non-executed fields of the R/3 structures    remain initial.


Structure: BGR00

__BEGIN_OF_RECORD__
BGR00 = INIT_BGR00.

BGR00-STYPE
  Rule Type:  Default Settings
    BGR00-STYPE = '0'.

BGR00-GROUP
  Rule Type:  Default Settings
    BGR00-GROUP = g_groupname.

BGR00-MANDT
  Rule Type:  Default Settings
    BGR00-MANDT = SY-MANDT.

BGR00-USNAM
  Rule Type:  Default Settings
    BGR00-USNAM = g_userid.
```

Figure 3.52: Object overview 3

Using the OVERVIEW OF REUSABLE RULES function (▦), you can display the rules for the fixed values, 1:1 translations, and user routines used (see Figure 3.53).

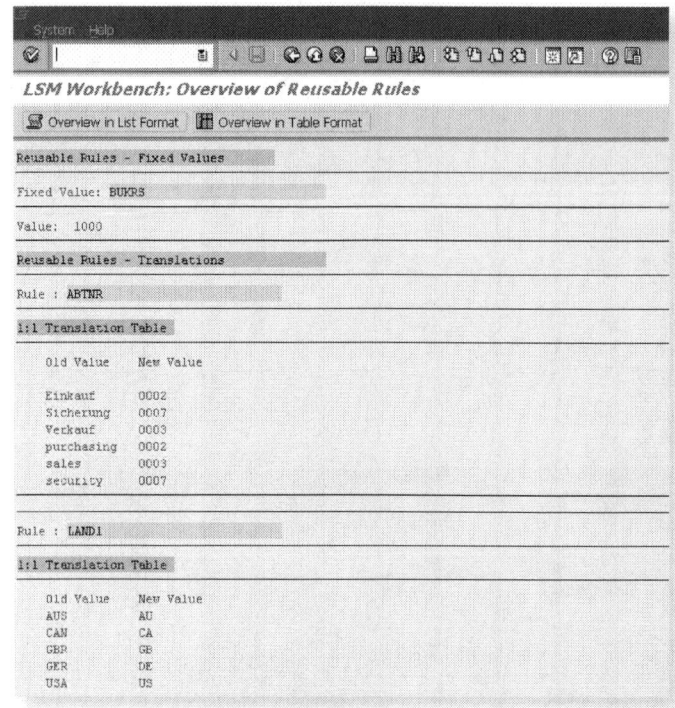

```
LSM Workbench: Overview of Reusable Rules
  Overview in List Format    Overview in Table Format

Reusable Rules - Fixed Values
Fixed Value: BUKRS
Value:  1000

Reusable Rules - Translations
Rule : ABTNR
1:1 Translation Table
    Old Value    New Value
    Einkauf      0002
    Sicherung    0007
    Verkauf      0003
    purchasing   0002
    sales        0003
    security     0007

Rule : LAND1
1:1 Translation Table
    Old Value    New Value
    AUS          AU
    CAN          CA
    GBR          GB
    GER          DE
    USA          US
```

Figure 3.53: Object overview 4

4 Recordings

You can use recordings to create a new object or a new import method. You can also use them to change and to create data. In most cases, they are used if none of the three standard import technologies are available for a data object, that is, there is no standard batch/direct input program and the BAPI and IDoc methods cannot be used. However, even if standard programs are available, recordings can be very useful to reduce the number of target fields.

In Chapter 3, I presented all of the important process steps for an LSMW data migration in detail. We used the import technology STANDARD BATCH/DIRECT INPUT and, using batch input program RFBIDE00, created a batch input session. By processing this session, we created new customer master records in the SAP system.

In this section, I will show you an example of how to create a *recording* and then use it in the LSM Workbench.

In our new example, we will change material master data. To do this we could also use the standard object 0020 (material master) with the underlying standard batch input program RMDATIND. However, as the change we want to make is only minimal (in our case a change to two fields), the recording method is much more effective here. For minimal changes, the mass maintenance transaction MASS is also useful. However, as not all fields required for a change are always available with this technology (in particular, user-defined enhancements), a recording is often the quickest and easiest way of achieving the objective.

Imagine the following situation: you want to change the shipping information for a group of materials. The changes concern the values for the loading group and the transport group. An Excel file with the corresponding material numbers and the information at the organizational level is already available (see Figure 4.1).

A	B	C	D	E	F
Material	Loading Group	Transportation Group	Plant	Sales Organization	Distribution Channel
1481	0003	0914	0001	0001	01
1482	0001	0913	0001	0001	01
1483	0003	0001	0001	0001	01
1484	0002	0914	0001	0001	01
1485	0003	0004	0001	0001	01
1486	0004	0914	0001	0001	01

Figure 4.1: Material numbers file

Before performing any changes, you should familiarize yourself with the transaction for changing material masters (MM02) and know exactly which views have to be selected and which fields have to be filled out.

In our case, all of the required information is already defined in the correct format and in the correct SAP terminology in the material numbers file, meaning that we do not require a mapping table at this point. Thus we can proceed directly with creating the recording.

4.1 Creating Recordings

To create or edit a recording, navigate to the LSMW initial screen (see Figure 2.3). In the menu bar, choose GOTO • RECORDINGS. As a recording is always created at project level, you have to enter at least the project name (see Figure 4.2). For our second example, I have created a new project including subproject name and object name, following the extensive description in Section 2.5:

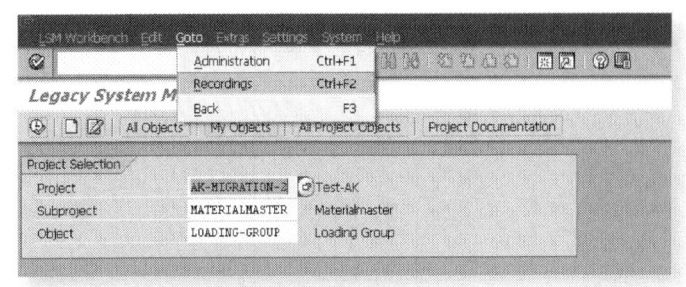

Figure 4.2: Creating recordings 1

An overview now appears, and should contain all recordings for the current project (see Figure 4.3). However, as we have not yet created any recordings for the project "AK-Migration-2," the overview is currently empty.

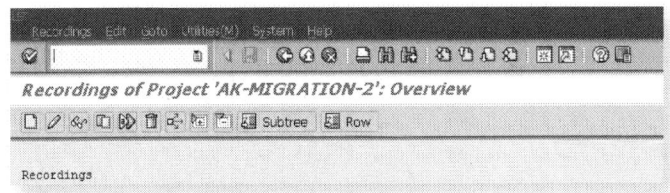

Figure 4.3: Creating recordings 2

On this overview screen, when you click CREATE RECORDING (), the dialog box shown in Figure 4.4 opens. Assign appropriate names for the fields RECORDING and DESCRIPTION and confirm the entries with ENTER ().

Figure 4.4: Creating recordings 3

In the next step, the system prompts you to enter the transaction code (see Figure 4.5).

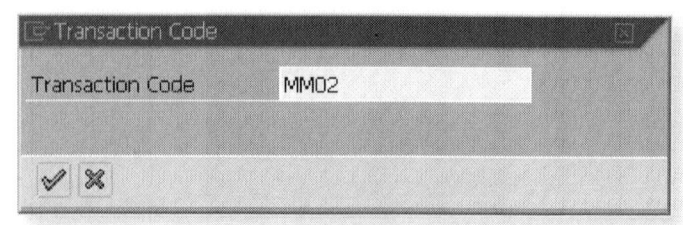

Figure 4.5: Entering the transaction code

To change the material master, enter transaction code MM02 and click CONTINUE ( ).

The system switches to the corresponding transaction, and you can enter the information required. Note that these entries are not merely simulated; they are actually executed and thus posted in the system. We are making changes for material 1481 which is at the top of our material numbers file (see Figure 4.1). You can see all of the entries required in Figures 4.6 to 4.9 below.

First enter material number 1481 and confirm the entry (see Figure 4.6):

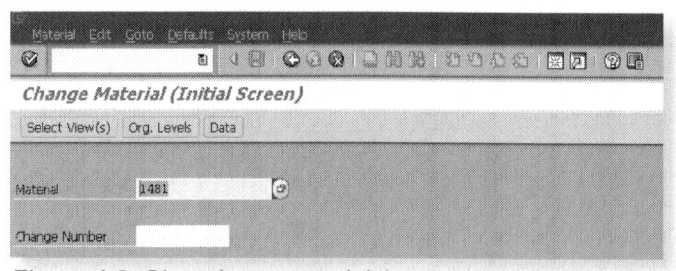

Figure 4.6: Changing a material 1

For all further changes to material masters, a *view selection* is then available. Before creating the recording, it is advisable to be clear about which views really need to be changed. The fewer views selected, the clearer the recording will be later on. We already know that the sales and distribution information to be changed in our example is located in the SALES: GENERAL/PLANT DATA view, and so we select only this entry (see Figure 4.7) and confirm the entry with ENTER.

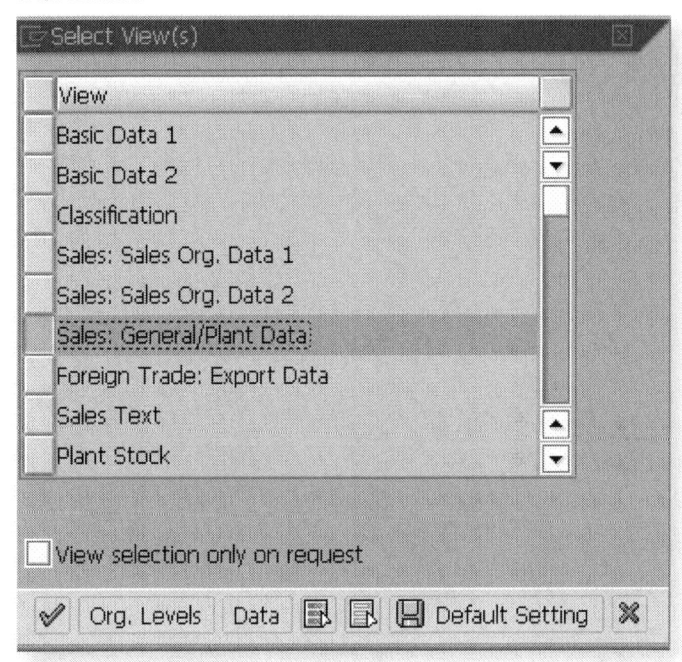

Figure 4.7: Changing a material 2

As our data to be changed is at the sales organization level, we also have to enter the corresponding organizational data (see Figure 4.8).

Figure 4.8: Changing a material 3

Figure 4.9: Changing a material 4 shows the fields to be changed in our example: TRANSPORT GROUP (TRANS. GRP) **1** and LOADING GROUP (LOADINGGRP) **2**.

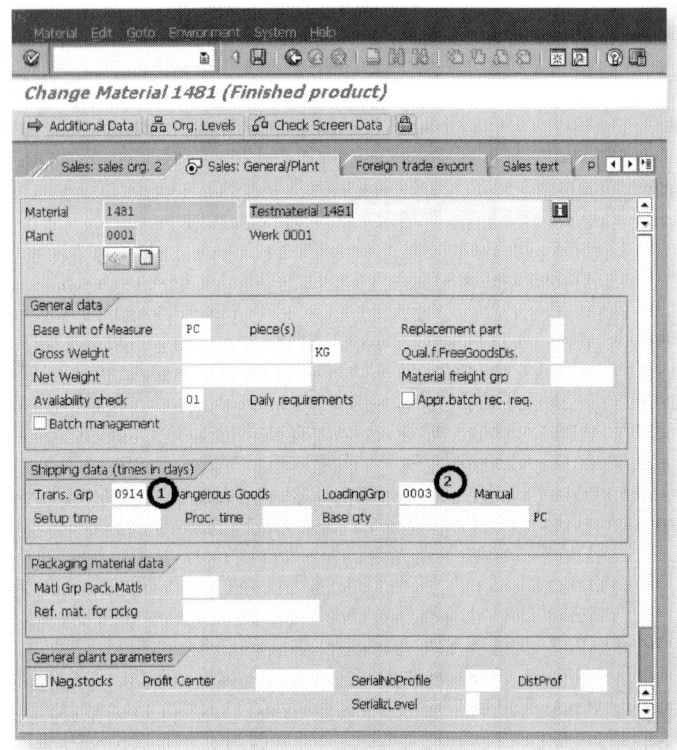

Figure 4.9: Changing a material 4

Saving the entries (🖫) triggers a change to the material master. It ends the work in the transaction and takes us to the tree display of the recording details shown in Figure 4.10.

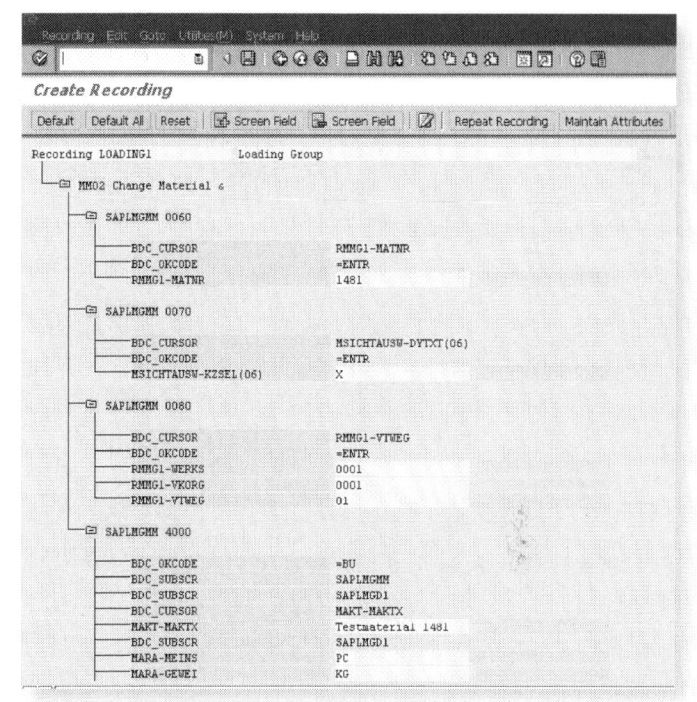

Figure 4.10: Material recording

Note that the recording is not created in the SAP system until the data is saved on this screen and after the issue of the message that the data was successfully saved. Before I address further input options in this overview below, I will briefly explain what is shown in Figure 4.10: the figure shows the technical components of the recording. These are the transaction name (MM02), the individual screens processed (SAPLMGMM 0060, 0070, 0080, and 4000) and the fields in which we entered information or which were already filled (RMMG1-MATNR etc.).

The display is arranged in three columns: in the middle column, the fields in which we made changes during the recording, or which already contained default values, are highlighted in color. The column to the right (highlighted in pink on the screen) is still empty and must now be filled with the field names of the target structure. To do this, position the cursor on the first input field (screen field RMMG1_MATNR, field content 1481). Double-click the entry to navigate to the dialog box shown in Figure 4.11, where you can assign both a short and a long name (in the system, both fields are called NAME) for the field, delete the default value and click CONTINUE (✓). These entries will appear later in the target structure.

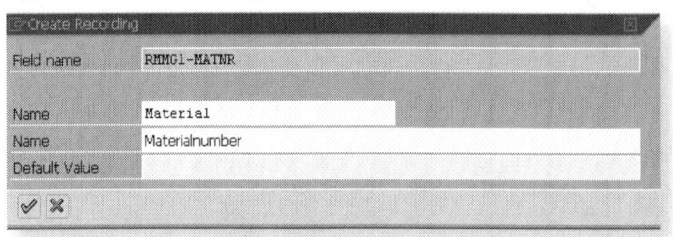

Create Recording	
Field name	RMMG1-MATNR
Name	Material
Name	Materialnumber
Default Value	

Figure 4.11: Creating recordings 4

For all input fields supplied with information from the legacy file (see the file in Figure 4.2), you have to make corresponding specifications.

However, the other fields, which contain default values, must also be analyzed. LSMW automatically adopts the defined default values for these provided we have not deleted them. Therefore, at this point, check very carefully whether these values are really valid for all data records that you want to import. For example, the material name (field MAKT-MAKTX): in our recording, a default value TESTMATERIAL 1481 was entered in this field:

| MAKT-MAKTX | Testmaterial 1481 |

If you do not change this, all materials from our legacy file will receive this name in the SAP system after processing by the LSMW!

To avoid this, the corresponding field must be removed from the recording using 🗔 Screen Field . Therefore, in our recording, I delete all defaulted fields except for PLANT, SALES ORGANIZATION, and DISTRIBUTION CHANNEL. To show you how this works, I will not read these fields from the legacy data; instead, I will use the default value, as all materials for our example are assigned to the same organizational structure.

For technical reasons, at least one field must have a NAME and a DESCRIPTION. Therefore, you cannot use a recording in which only defaulted values are imported.

After creating the field names and descriptions for MATERIAL NUMBER, TRANSPORT GROUP, and LOADING GROUP, the result is as shown in Figure 4.12. You can access this compressed display via UTILITIES • CHANGE LAYOUT.

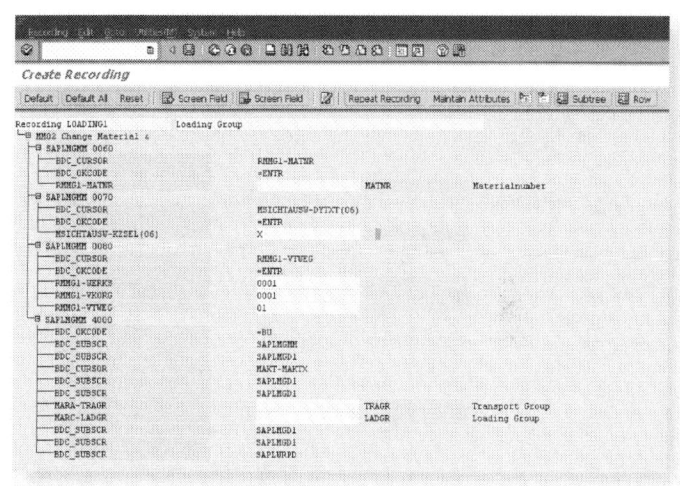

Figure 4.12: Creating recordings 5

95

Figure 4.10 and Figure 4.12 show further buttons available. I will explain the most important ones briefly here:

▶ Default means that for the field on which the cursor is positioned, the SAP default name and the description are entered (for example, MATNR - Material Number).

▶ With Default All, the SAP system automatically sets the SAP name and description for all fields. This can save a lot of time. However, if you use this you should be familiar with SAP naming conventions, as these are not always "descriptive."

▶ Reset resets the entry for the field on which the cursor is positioned.

▶ You can use Add Screen Field ( ) to add one or more fields on a screen. To do this, place the cursor on the name of the corresponding screen (for example, SAPLMGMM 0080) and click Screen Field. A selection menu opens with all fields available on this screen and you can select any missing fields.

▶ Delete Screen Field ( ) deletes the selected field from the recording.

▶ You can use MAINTAIN ATTRIBUTES to change the name of the recording.

We now save the information we have entered so far and use the BACK button to return to the recording overview screen, which now looks as follows (see Figure 4.13):

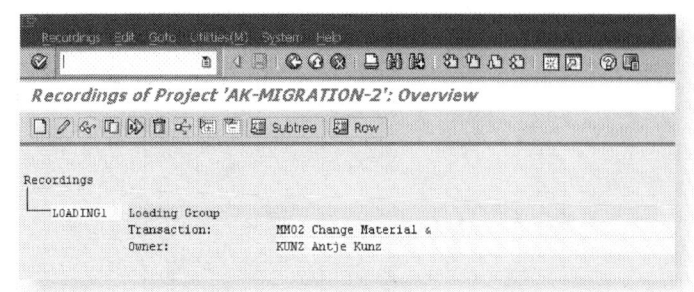

Figure 4.13: Creating recordings 6

4.2 Using the Recording Import Technology in the LSMW

We will now use the recording we have just created, specifically in the following items created in 4.1:

Project: AK-MIGRATION-2

Subproject: MATERIALMASTER

Object: LOADING-GROUP

Call up transaction LSMW, select the above-mentioned project information, and navigate to the overview screen shown in Figure 3.4.

Select the process step MAINTAIN OBJECT ATTRIBUTES by double-clicking it. Under OBJECT TYPE AND IMPORT METHOD, select BATCH INPUT RECORDINGS and, using the input help ( ), select our recording LOADING1 (see Figure 4.14). Here, only one recording is offered, as there currently is only one recording for the project AK-MIGRATION-2 (see also Figure 4.13).

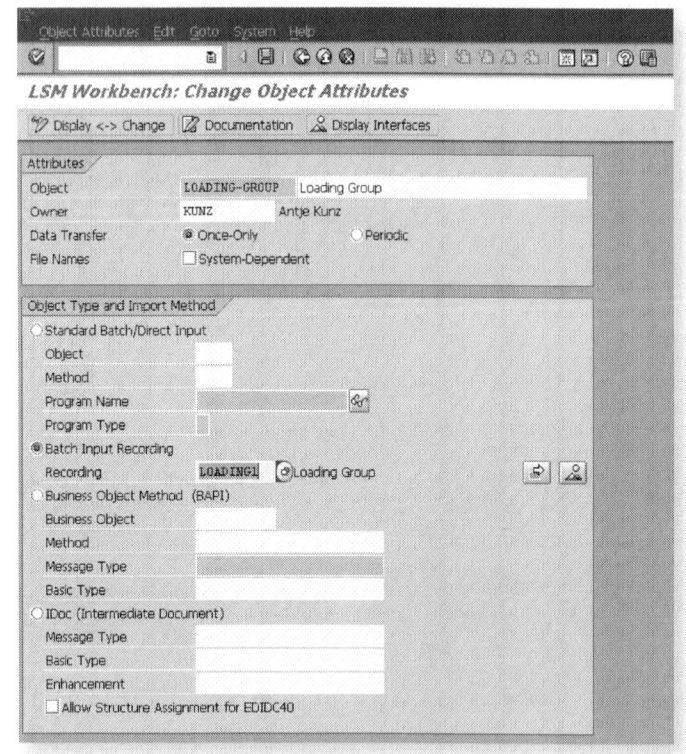

Figure 4.14: Object attributes — recordings

Via the FURTHER RECORDINGS button ( ), you can select and run multiple recordings. This allows you to process various transactions on a data record one after the other. However, this function is rarely used.

Via RECORDING(S) • OVERVIEW ( ), you can access the overview screen for the recording (see Figure 4.13) and can view or change the selected recording.

We save the entries in the object attribute maintenance and proceed to the next process step MAINTAIN SOURCE STRUCTURES. This was described in detail in Section 3.3. There I stated that for user-specific objects (created by a recording), only one structure may be defined. This simplifies this process step considerably, as we only have to create one source structure. For our example we call it SOURCE with the description SOURCESTRUCTURE and save the entries.

In the next process step we define the source fields. Corresponding to the legacy data file, we create the source fields MATERIAL, LOADING GROUP, and TRANSPORT GROUP and save the entries. The result is shown in Figure 4.15.

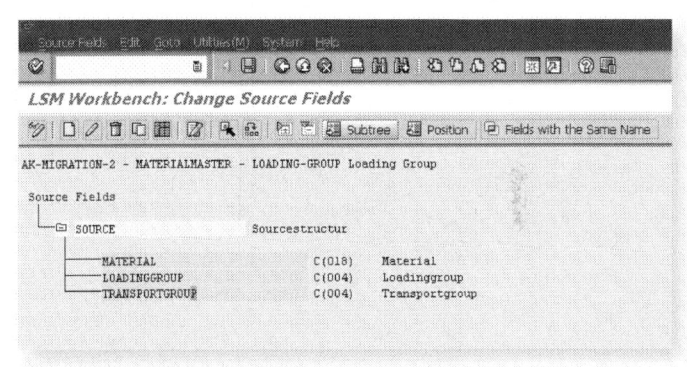

Figure 4.15: Source fields — recording

The next process step MAINTAIN STRUCTURE RELATIONSHIPS is very easy as there is only one source and one target structure. The system creates the assignment automatically (see Figure 4.16) and you just have to confirm this proposal.

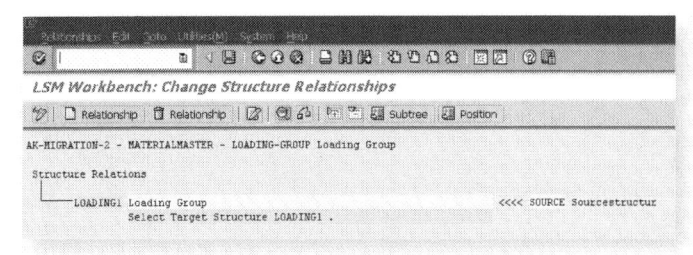

Figure 4.16: Structure relationship — recording

Now we come to the process step Maintain Field Mapping and Conversion Rules. In Sect 3.6, I described this step as very time-consuming. In our case however, it is very simple, as we only have to map three fields 1:1: Material Number, Transport Group, and Loading Group (see Figure 4.17).

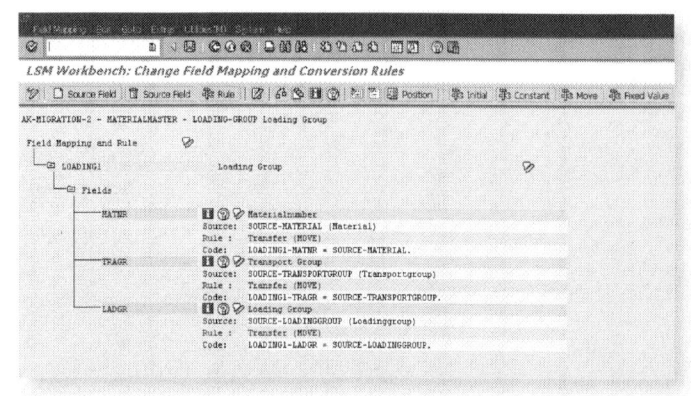

Figure 4.17: Field mapping — recording

As we do not use or create any fixed values, translations, or user-defined routines in this example, we can skip this process step and proceed directly to Specify Files. We read the legacy data as usual from the frontend PC and use the same settings as described in Section 3.8. Here too we have to shorten the name of the converted file and the result is as shown in Figure 4.18.

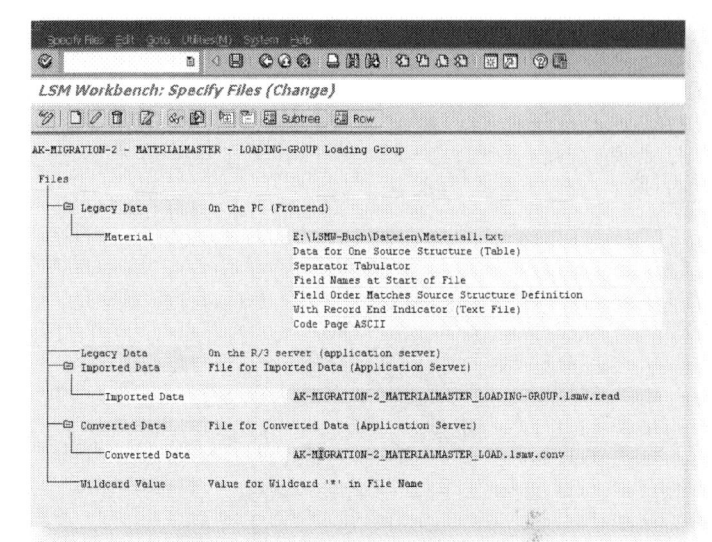

Figure 4.18: Specifying files — recording

The LSM Workbench step Assign Files (see Figure 4.19) is also very easy, and we can now start the step Read Data.

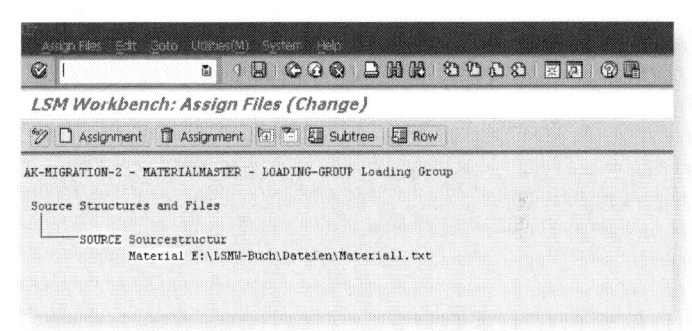

Figure 4.19: Assigning files — recording

The subsequent process steps Read Data, Display Read Data, and Convert Data are already described in detail in Sections 3.10 to 3.13 and are not explained again here, as the procedure is identical.

Although the next process step CREATE BATCH INPUT SESSION has already been described in Section 3.14, I will explain it again more closely here. As you can see in Figure 4.20, SAP proposes the name of the file in accordance with our previous example, AK-Migration-1. However, all other fields are fundamentally different to those in Figure 3.44. This is because in this example, we are using transaction MM02 to change the material masters and thus using a different BTCI program, which creates the selection options shown in Figure 4.20.

In particular, refer to Section 3.14 for the ☐ Keep batch input folder(s)? function described there. If you select this field, after processing, the session remains in the BATCH INPUT SESSION OVERVIEW (transaction SM35). This means that you can analyze it and use it for audit purposes. It is not possible to process the session twice by accident.

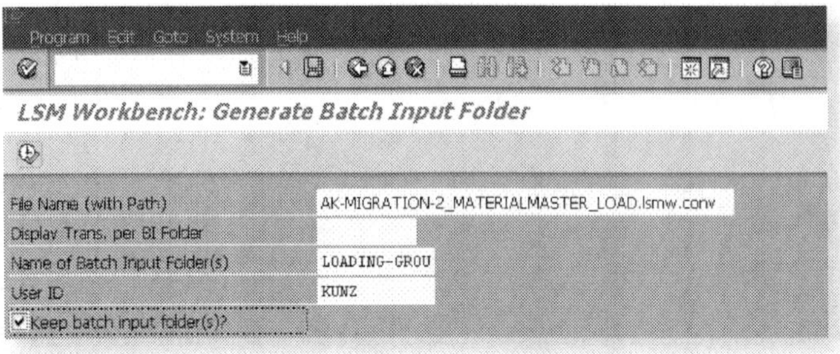

Figure 4.20: Creating a BTCI — recording

In this overview you can also change the USER ID. This is particularly useful for the final creation of the BTCI session(s) in the live environment. Here you can enter the name of the business employee who is to import/change the data. This employee often only has authorization for sessions with his own user ID.

Do not forget that you can limit the number of transactions per batch input session (Display Trans. per BI Folder). This is particularly recommended for large volumes of data.

Now we come to the last process step, RUN BATCH INPUT SESSION. To enable a better analysis of the operations in the system, I have only imported one data record and run it in the foreground, meaning that each screen entry executed can be followed (see Figure 4.21 and Figure 4.22).

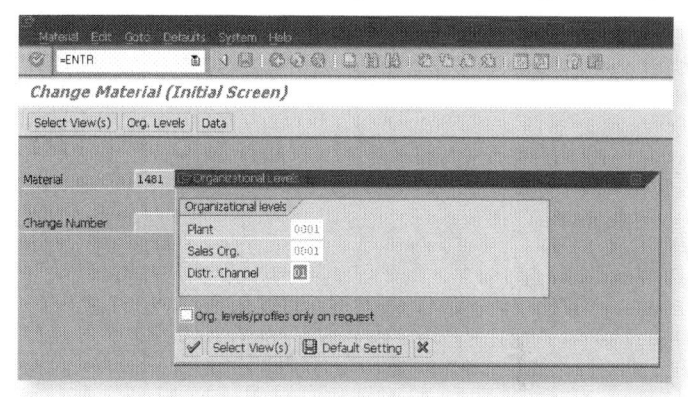

Figure 4.21: Processing session 1

In Figure 4.21, you can see that organizational level fields with default values in the recording are filled automatically. The field content entered or changed is highlighted in color accordingly (here red).

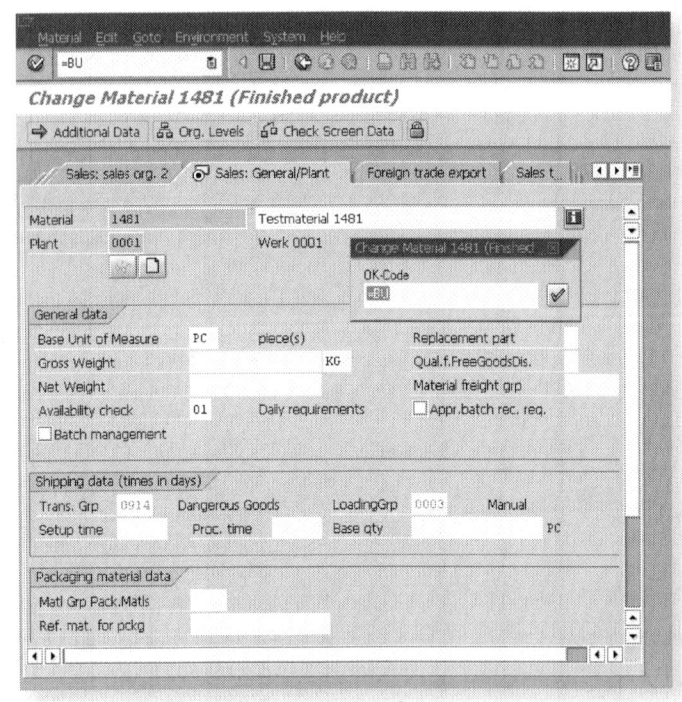

Figure 4.22: Processing session 2

In Figure 4.22, Transport Group and Loading Group are adopted from the legacy file. These are the only fields highlighted in color on this screen and we can be sure that other fields (such as the material text) are not changed accidentally.

You can end the processing of the session with Enter or OK Code =BU.

As we selected in Figure 4.20 that the BTCI session should be retained, it is still available on the Processed tab.

In this chapter, you have learned how to work with the import method BATCH INPUT RECORDING. I hope I have been able to convince you that this method has many advantages, particularly for simple data transfers/changes, as it is very quick to create and to apply.

5 LSMW Using BAPI and IDoc Import Technology

In this chapter I will give you a brief overview of BAPIs and IDocs and explain in detail how to create orders in LSMW using the *Business Object Method (BAPI)* import technology.

I will assume that you already have a basic understanding of this topic as to explain it completely would exceed the scope of this book.

For illustration purposes, I will use the materials changed in Chapter 4 via BATCH INPUT RECORDING. The customer masters created in Chapter 3 using the DIRECT INPUT METHOD cannot be used here as, due to the simplification of the example, they are assigned to a customer group that is not suitable for this task and were also not created at sales area level.

At the end of this chapter, you should be able to check the prerequisites for use of the BAPI and IDoc method, configure it yourself if necessary, and create LSM Workbench projects based on this import technology.

5.1 General Definitions

▶ BAPI:

"To enable technical integration and the exchange of business data between SAP components and between SAP and non-SAP components, SAP created the Business Framework. An important part of the Business Framework is the Business Application Programming Interfaces (BAPIs). They represent the visible interfaces at the component boundaries and as a result of their properties, they ensure the integration of these components.

This integration can comprise both components within a local network and components that are connected with one another via the Internet.

BAPIs enable an integration at the business level rather than at the technical level. This provides for greater stability of the linkage and independence from the underlying communication technology used."

Source: help.sap.com — General Introduction to BAPIs (CA-BFA)

▶ IDoc

The IDoc (Intermediate Document) is a container for exchanging data between different SAP systems and between SAP systems and external systems. IDoc processing is used within the LSM Workbench as a standard interface for data transfer.

5.2 Basic Settings for Using BAPIs and IDocs

To enable you to use the import technologies BAPI and IDoc in the LSM Workbench, you have to configure the settings shown below once in the SAP system for each client and project.

On the LSMW initial screen, select SETTINGS • IDOC INBOUND PROCESSING and confirm the selection with ENTER (see Figure 5.1).

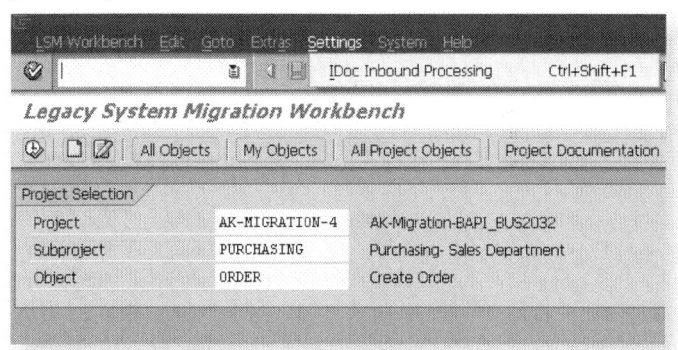

Figure 5.1: IDoc/BAPI preparation

The screen shown in Figure 5.2, IDOC INBOUND PROCESSING: PREPARATORY MEASURES, opens.

LSMW USING BAPI AND IDOC

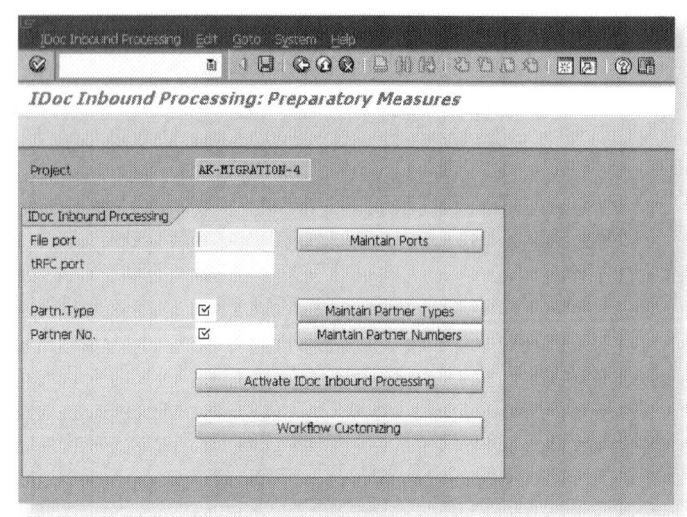

Figure 5.2: Preparatory measures

Here you have to enter or create the FILE PORT, PARTNER TYPE, and PARTNER NUMBER as mandatory information.

Click MAINTAIN PORTS to navigate to an overview screen with the previously maintained ports in the IDoc processing. For the data transfer, we need a port of the type FILE. This is created as follows (see also Figure 5.3):

▶ Port: LSMW

▶ Description: Legacy System Migration Workbench

▶ Version: IDoc record types SAP release 4.X

▶ Physical Directory: Enter a file path and name — in our example: /USR/SAP/I62/SYS/GLOBAL/

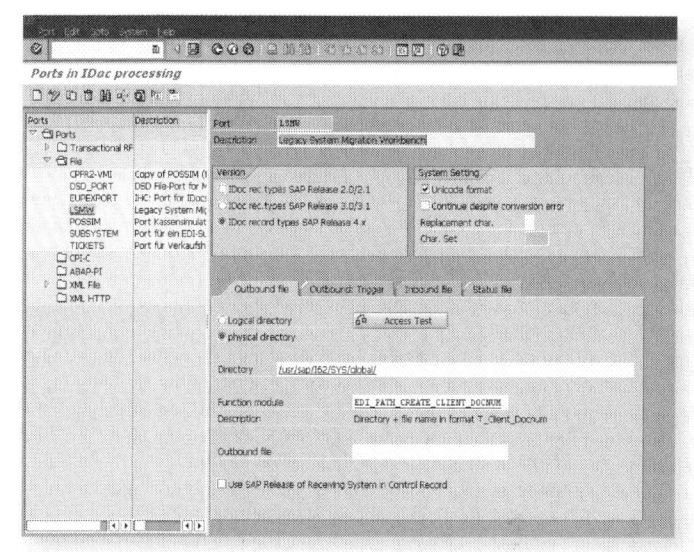

Figure 5.3: IDoc — maintaining the file port

In a next step, starting from the IDoc inbound processing screen (see Figure 5.2), you can use Maintain Partner Types to enter the code that identifies the commercial relationship between the recipient and the sender. Here, following the recommendations from SAP, you should enter "US." This partner type is available in the standard system from SAP Release 4.5A. If you are working with an older release status without "US," adopt the settings for the following as shown in Figure 5.4: PARTNER TYPE, REPORT NAME, FORM ROUTINE, and SHORT TEXT.

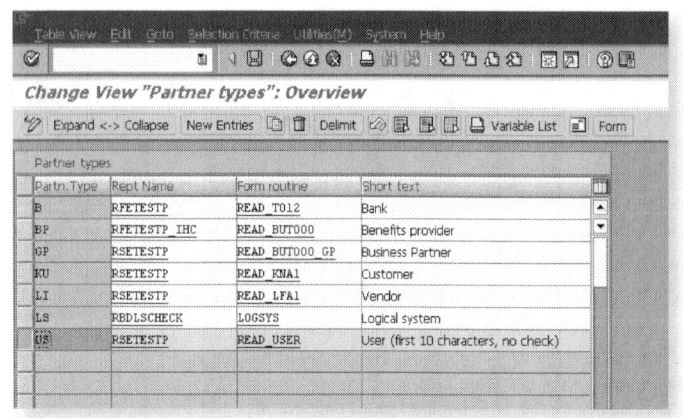

Figure 5.4: IDoc — maintaining the partner type

The last mandatory entry of the *preparatory measures* is the partner number. To configure this entry, in Figure 5.2 click MAINTAIN PARTNER NUMBERS and, if it has not yet been created in your system, enter the following information (see Figure 5.5):

▶ Partner Number: LSMW

▶ Partner Type: US

▶ Type: US

▶ Agent: Your user ID

▶ Language: DE or EN

▶ Partner Status: A (active) — on the CLASSIFICATION tab

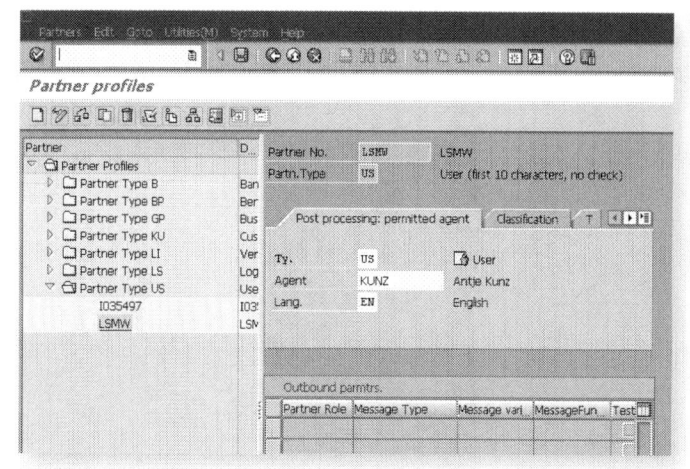

Figure 5.5: IDoc — partner agreements

Once you have entered this information, you have to activate the IDoc inbound processing. To do this, click ACTIVATE IDOC INBOUND PROCESSING in Figure 5.2 and confirm the question of whether you want to activate event linkage with YES.

The preparatory measures are completed with the WORKFLOW CUSTOMIZING, which you have to perform once for each system. To do this, click `Workflow Customizing` on the overview screen (see Figure 5.2).

The following settings (see Figure 5.6) are recommended:

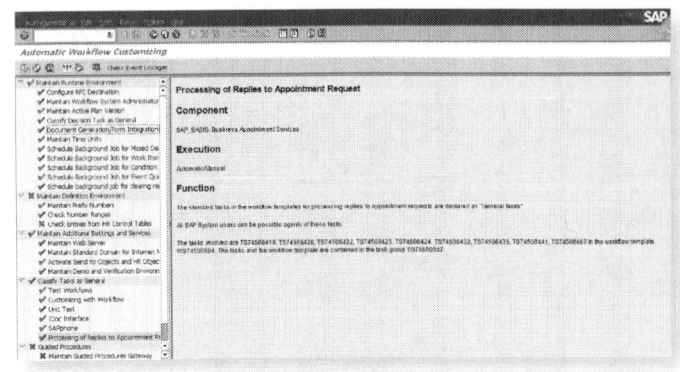

Figure 5.6: Workflow Customizing

5.3 Creating Orders Using the BAPI Technology

Now that we have successfully completed the preparatory measures for IDoc inbound processing, I will explain working with the BAPI import technology in more detail using an example.

The main objective is to create orders in SAP using LSMW and the BAPI import technology.

I have already created the example project "AK-Migration-4" with subproject and object in Section 5.2 (see Figure 5.1), hence we can start to maintain the attributes in LSMW straight away.

To work with the BAPI method, we need a BUSINESS OBJECT, the METHOD, and the BASIC TYPE (see Figure 5.7). You will already know these details or you can search for them via the input help or using transaction BAPI. In the excursus below I will address this transaction in more detail.

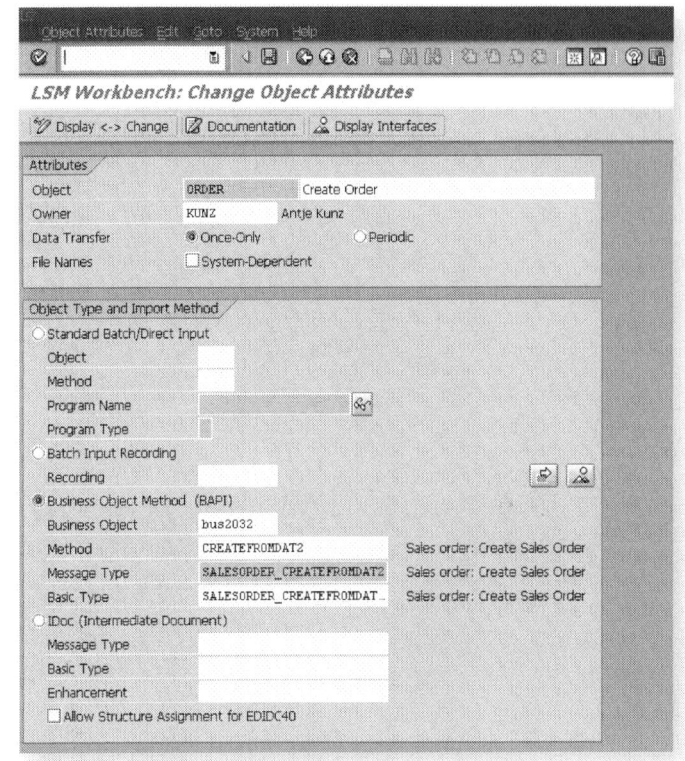

Figure 5.7: Maintaining BAPI object attributes

As we want to create orders in our example, we can use the business object BUS2032 (SALES ORDER).

Excursus: Here I will briefly demonstrate how you can search for business objects and methods and find important information about them.

The transaction BAPI is very useful here — you can find it in the SAP menu under TOOLS • ABAP WORKBENCH • OVERVIEW • APPLICATION HIERARCHY • BAPI (see Figure 5.8).

115

LSMW USING BAPI AND IDOC

```
▽ 📁 Tools
    ▽ 📁 ABAP Workbench
        ▽ 📁 Overview
            ▷ 📁 Application Hierarchy
               ⊙ SE80 - Object Navigator
               ⊙ SWO2 - Business Object Browser
               ⊙ SE95 - Modification Browser
               ⊙ SE83 - Reuse Library
               ⊙ SE84 - Information System
               ⊙ SE16 - Data Browser
               ⊙ SE09 - Transport Organizer
               ⊙ BAPI - BAPI Explorer
```

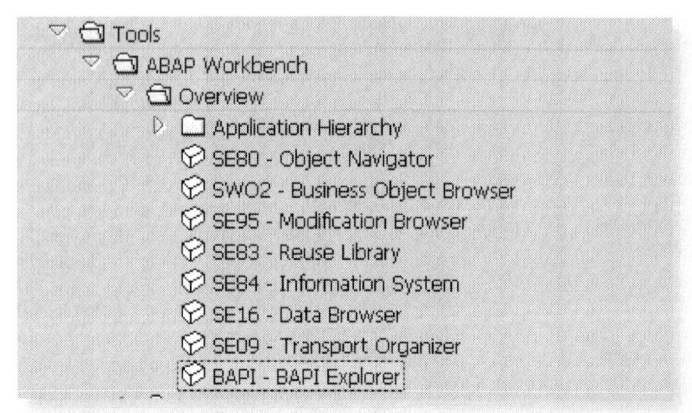

Figure 5.8: Transaction BAPI

We can use this transaction to access the BAPI Explorer. On the left-hand side of the screen, we can view the existing BAPIs arranged hierarchically or alphabetically or, via EDIT • FIND, we can search by object name and/or object type (see Figure 5.9).

As we want to create sales orders in our example, we search for SALESORDER and discover that there is an object type BUS2032 for this. We also need information about the METHOD. We can find this by opening the subitems for ▽ ⊙ SalesOrder on the left-hand side of the screen and looking at the individual BAPI methods more closely. For our example, the method CREATEFROMDAT2 is the most suitable. On the DOCUMENTATION tab, you will find more information about this method, including which fields have to be filled (see Figure 5.10). For our example, I have concentrated on the required entry fields, to keep the number of entries required as low as possible.

LSMW Using BAPI and IDoc

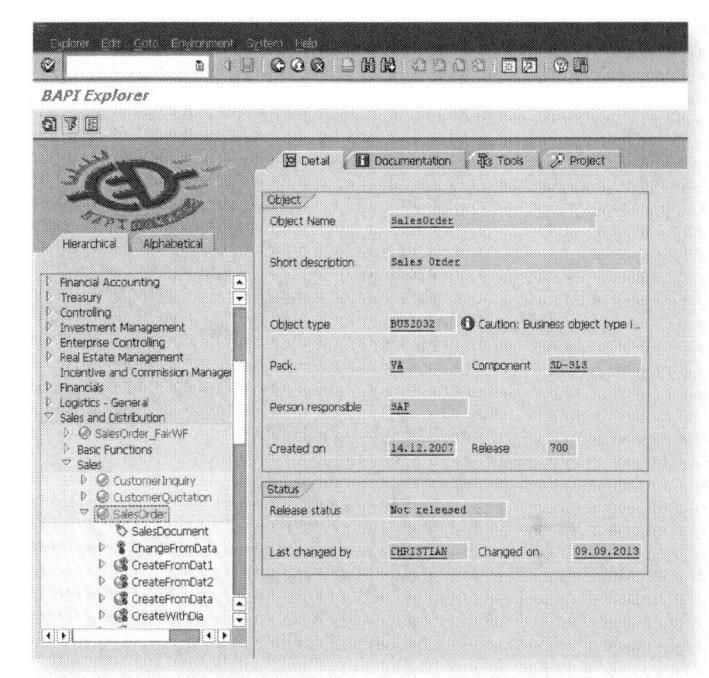

Figure 5.9: BAPI Explorer

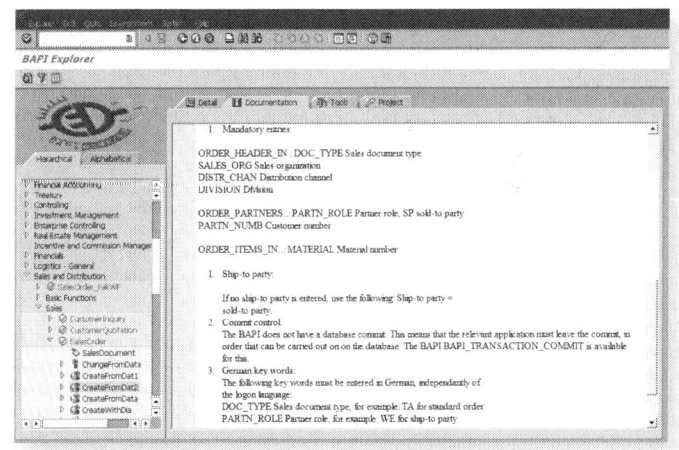

Figure 5.10: BAPI Explorer documentation

We will now return to our starting point, maintaining the BAPI object attributes.

The BASIC TYPE is still missing, and we can determine this via the input help.

We select SALESORDER_CREATEFROMDAT202.

After completing the attribute maintenance, save the entries and return to the LSMW overview screen. Due to the import technology selected, this is structured as follows (see Figure 5.11):

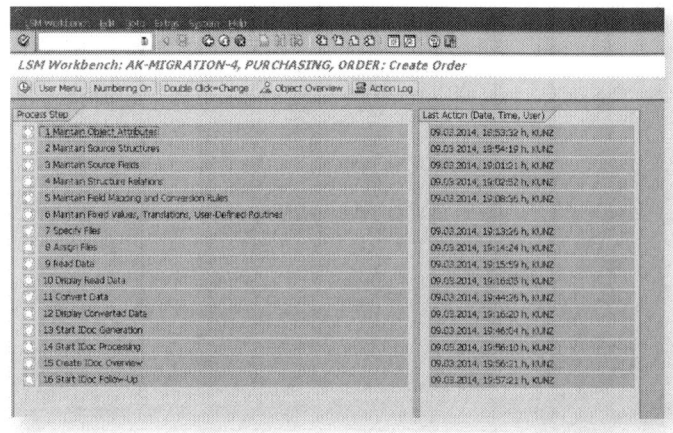

Figure 5.11: LSMW BAPI overview screen

We will now look at the next process step MAINTAIN SOURCE STRUCTURES. For this step, we need detailed information about the legacy data.

Our example consists of the header and item information (see Figure 5.12 and Figure 5.13):

	A	B	C	D	E	F	G
1	IDENTIFIER	AUART	VKORG	VTWEG	SPART	KUNNR	ROLE
2	A	TA	0001	01	01	0000021099	AG
3							

Figure 5.12: Order header

	A	B	C	D	E
1	IDENTIFIER	MATNR	KWMENG	KMEIN	PTYP
2	A	000000000000001483	4	ST	TAN
3					

Figure 5.13: Order item

Therefore, we create the source structures as follows (see Figure 5.14):

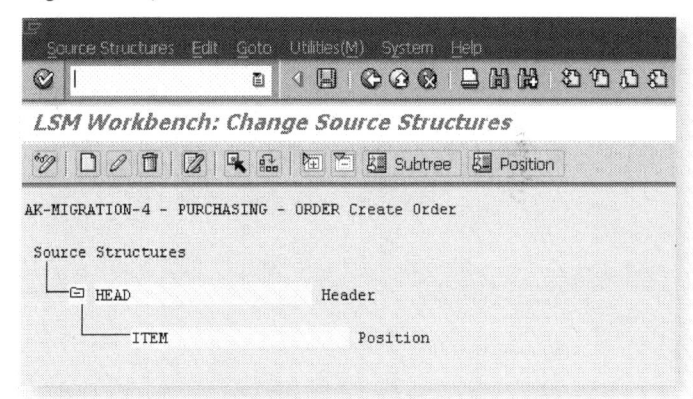

Figure 5.14: Creating the BAPI source structures

In the third process step, the source fields are created according to Figure 5.15:

LSMW USING BAPI AND IDOC

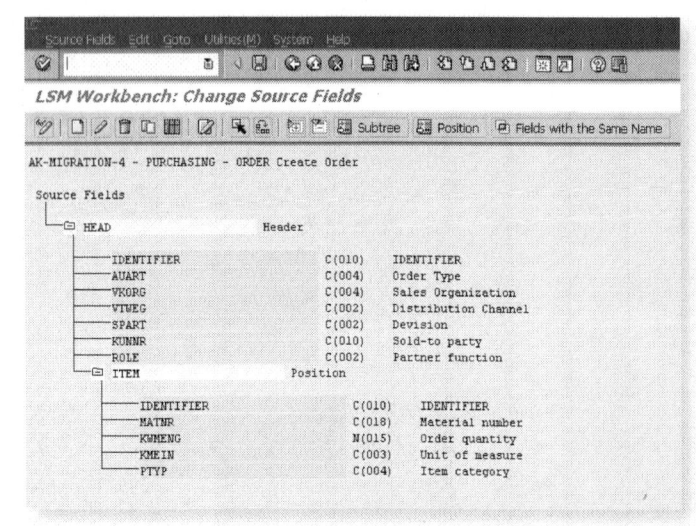

Figure 5.15: Creating the BAPI source fields

The subsequent maintenance of the structure relationships is shown in Figure 5.16:

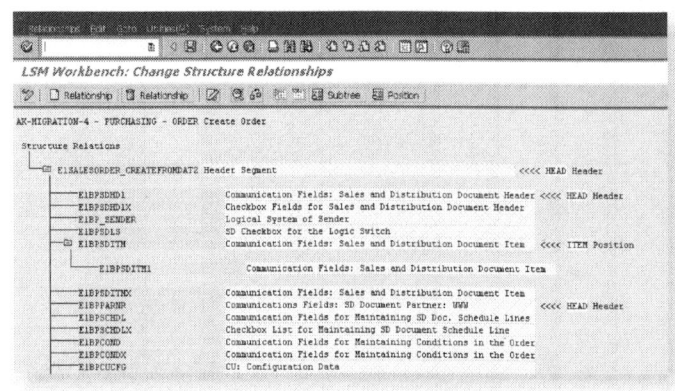

Figure 5.16: BAPI structure relationships

The options in the subsequent process step MAINTAIN FIELD MAPPING AND CONVERSION RULES were described in detail in Section 3.6. In this example, I have created a 1:1 assignment between source and target fields, and this is shown in Figure 5.17 and Figure 5.18.

LSMW USING BAPI AND IDOC

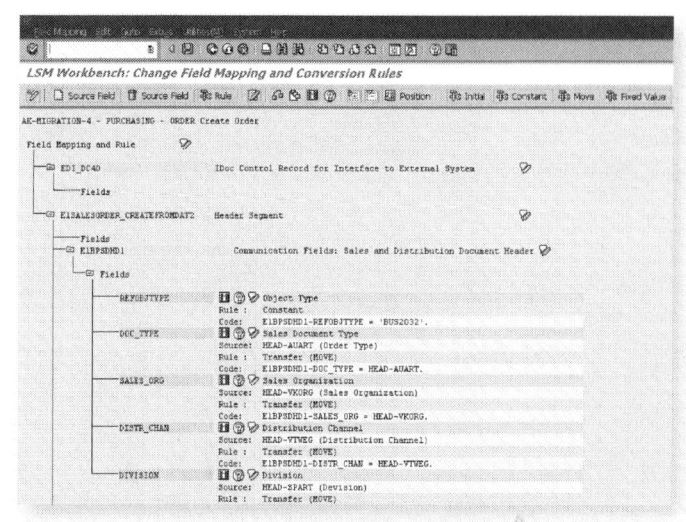

Figure 5.17: BAPI field mapping 1

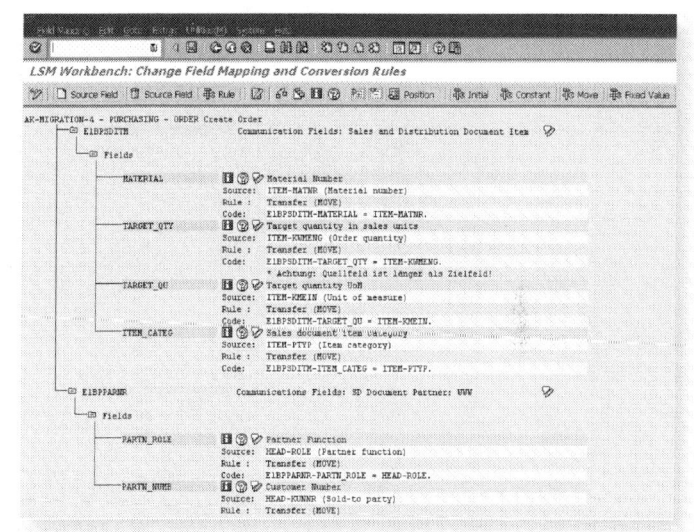

Figure 5.18: BAPI field mapping 2

Process step 6 shown in Figure 5.11 (MAINTAIN FIXED VALUES, TRANSLATIONS, USER-DEFINED ROUTINES) can be omitted here, and we can go directly to SPECIFY FILES. Both source files (see Figure 5.12 and Figure 5.13) are converted into the TXT format and assigned accordingly (see Figure 5.19).

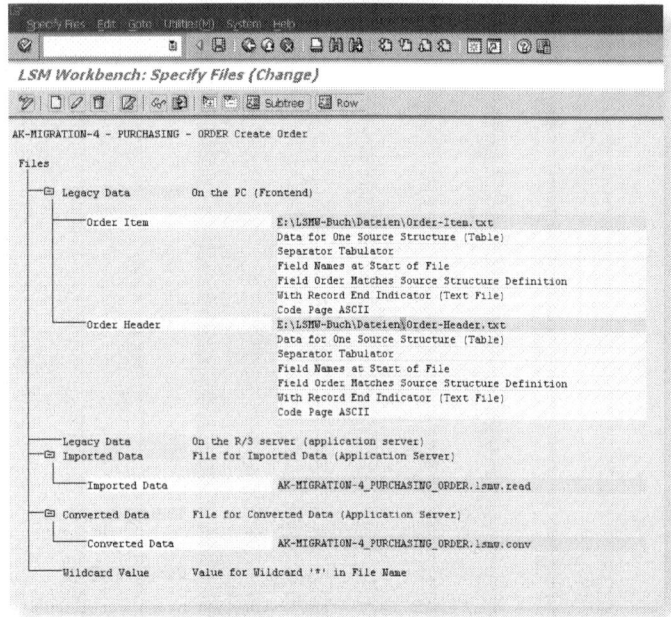

Figure 5.19: Specifying BAPI files

Figure 5.20 shows the assignment of the files as the next process step. The data is then read and converted.

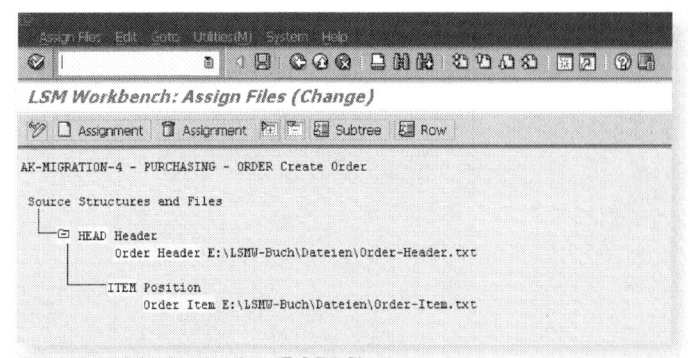

Figure 5.20: Assigning BAPI files

Process step 13 in *Figure 5.11* transfers the previously selected file

AK-MIGRATION-4_PURCHASING_ORDER.LSMW.CONV

for IDOC GENERATION, and you then receive the information shown in Figure 5.21, which you can confirm with ENTER.

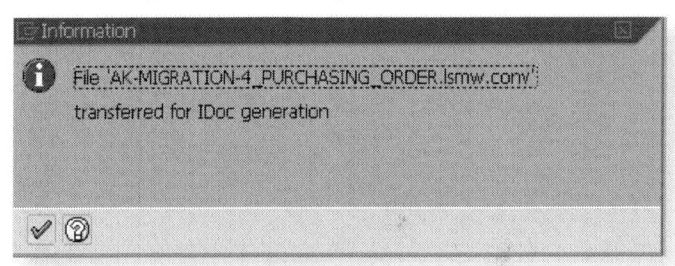

Figure 5.21: BAPI/IDoc transfer

When you execute process step 14, START IDOC PROCESSING (see Figure 5.22), the IDocs are processed in the system and you receive an overview of the IDocs transferred to the application, including status information. This is shown in Figure 5.23.

LSMW Using BAPI and IDoc

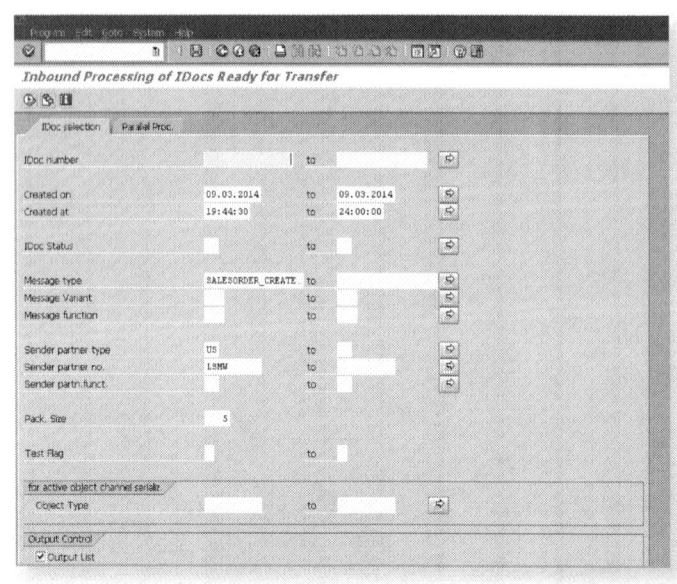

Figure 5.22: IDoc processing

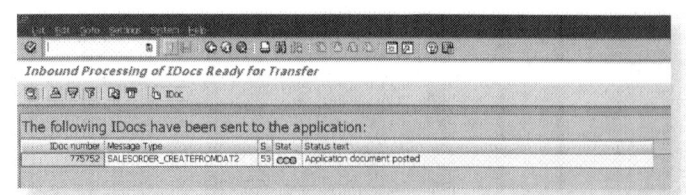

Figure 5.23: IDoc inbound processing

By double-clicking the IDoc number in Figure 5.23, you receive detailed information showing that we have successfully posted order 13101 (see Figure 5.24).

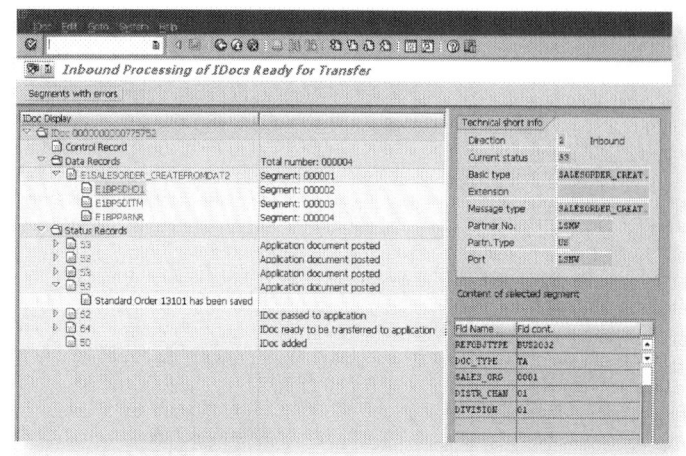

Figure 5.24: IDoc details

You can also display corresponding information using transaction WE02.

This ends the actual LSMW processing with BAPI and, providing processing was successful, the data was created or changed. In process step 15, CREATE IDOC OVERVIEW, you receive a status overview with all IDocs created.

If IDocs created could not be posted, postprocessing is possible in the process step START IDOC FOLLOW-UP. Note the IDoc number, as this will be queried when you enter information. For more information on this step, see the SAP Library.

6 Long Texts

The transfer of long texts has a special status in data migration. As this important topic is considered much too late in many projects, I am dedicating a separate chapter to it in this book.

6.1 Long Texts in SAP

Long texts are generally texts consisting of multiple lines that are used to exchange information. In the SAP system, they are stored in a separate text pool in the database. Therefore, long texts must also be migrated separately.

In the material master, long texts include inspection texts, basic data texts, internal comments, and purchase order texts. In sales and distribution, there are, for example, sales texts for a material or sales notes for a customer.

The key for a long text is composed of the following four parts:

- Object
- ID
- Name
- SPRAS

Table 6.1 lists these four key fields with their meaning, an example, the field length, and according to the respective check table.

Key field	Meaning	Example	Length	Check table
OBJECT	Application object	Material	10	TTXOB, TTXOT
ID	Text ID	PRUE	4	TTXID, TTXIT
NAME	Actual text key	000000000000001484 (18-character material number)	70	------
SPRAS	Language	DE	1-2	T002

Table 6.1: Long text key fields

The SAP system does not contain any standardized rules for the structure of the actual TEXT KEYS — key field NAME. As shown in Table 6.1, there is also no check table for this key field. However, if you want to maintain the structures and fields, you must know the structure of the text key and the values for TEXT ID and OBJECT. The example "Material inspection text" below will show you how to determine these:

1. Display the inspection text in the material master.
2. Using 📝, switch to the editor.
3. In the menu path of the text editor, choose GOTO • HEADER and access the desired information (see Figure 6.1).

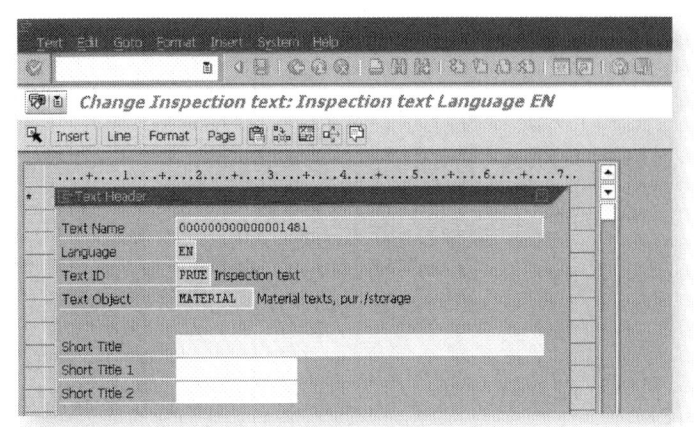

Figure 6.1: Displaying the text key

Thus we know the structure of the key fields and using an example, we can work through the individual process steps in the LSM Workbench.

The task this time is to create INSPECTION TEXTS, BASIC DATA TEXTS, and INTERNAL COMMENTS for the materials used in Chapter 4. For this purpose I have created the project AK-MIGRATION-5, with the subproject MATERIALMASTER, and the object LONGTEXT.

6.2 LSMW Objects for Long Texts

There are two options for transferring long texts, and both are based on direct input programs:

1. **Object 2000, method 0000** (direct input program RSTXLITF). To use this object, you have to download the transport from SAPNET (http://service.sap.com/LSMW) and import it into your system. For valuable tips on using this method and the structure of the inbound file, see the documentation for program RSTXLITF.

2. **Object 0001, method 0001** with the underlying program /SAPDMC/SAP_LSMW_IMPORT_TEXTS (see Figure 6.2). I will explain this method in detail in the following example. Note that it is not available in the standard system. To use it, you have to execute program /SAPDMC/SAP_LSMW_SXDA_TEXTS once.

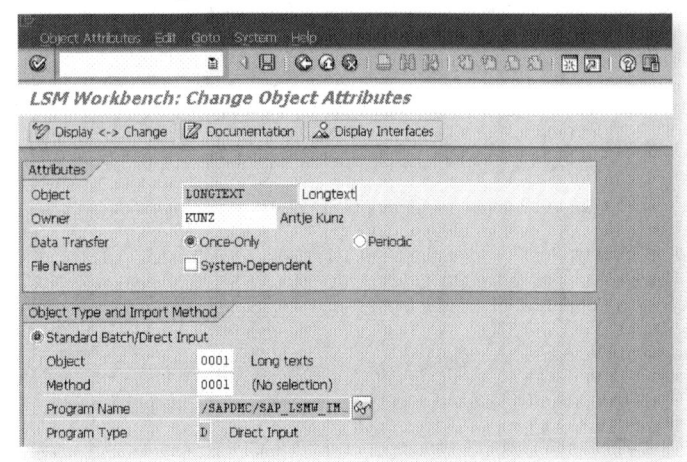

Figure 6.2: Long text — object attributes

Object type 0001 consists of the two target structures "long text header" and "long text line." I will describe the existing target fields and their meaning here, as we need this knowledge to set up the source structure and source fields.

Long text header — SAPDMC/LTXTH

- S<small>TYPE</small>: Record type (default value = 1)
- Object: Application object
- N<small>AME</small>: Text name
- ID: Text ID
- S<small>PRAS</small>: Language key

Long text line — SAPDMC/LTXTH

- S<small>TYPE</small>: Record type (default value = 2)
- T<small>EXT</small> F<small>ORMAT</small>: Tag column
- T<small>EXT</small> L<small>INE</small>: Text line

The field T<small>EXT</small> F<small>ORMAT</small> contains a format key for the output preparation for the text. This defines the beginning of a new text paragraph and the formatting for this paragraph. For a 1:1 transfer of the text, enter "*" in this field.

Based on this information, we compose a simple input file for the material long texts as follows (see Figure 6.3).

	A	B	C	D	E	F
1	Text-ID	Language	Object	Text-key	Text-Format	Text-Line
2	IVER	EN	MATERIAL	000000000000001484	*	internal comment
3	GRUN	EN	MATERIAL	000000000000001484	*	basic data text
4	PRUE	EN	MATERIAL	000000000000001484	*	inspection text line_1
5	PRUE	EN	MATERIAL	000000000000001484	*	inspection text line_2
6	PRUE	EN	MATERIAL	000000000000001484	*	inspection text line_3

Figure 6.3: Long text Excel file

6.3 Long Texts — Source Structures, Source Fields, Structure Relationships

I have summarized these first three LSMW process steps, which you know, and visualized them in Figure 6.4 to Figure 6.6:

```
LSM Workbench: Change Source Structures

AK-MIGRATION-5 - MATERIALMASTER - LONGTEXT Longtext

Source Structures
    └── TEXT                    File with Longtext
```

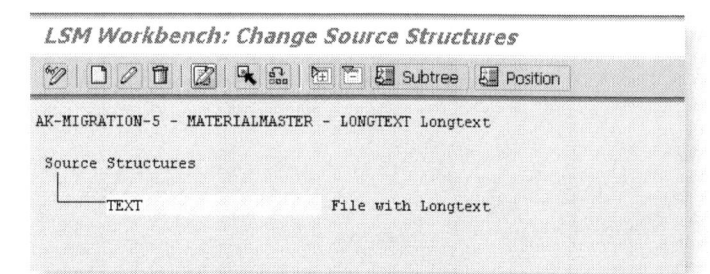

Figure 6.4: Long text — source structures

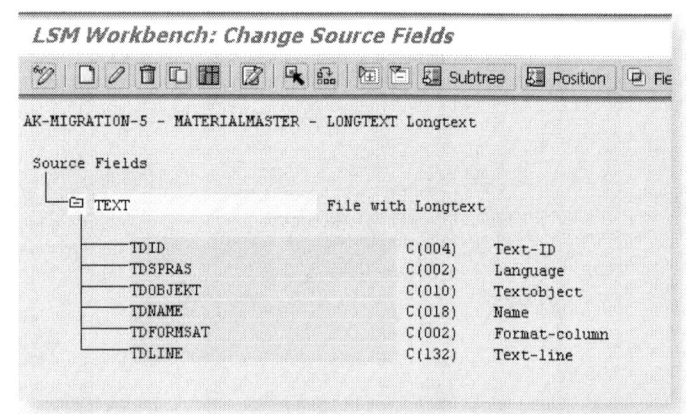

```
LSM Workbench: Change Source Fields

AK-MIGRATION-5 - MATERIALMASTER - LONGTEXT Longtext

Source Fields
    └──📁 TEXT                    File with Longtext
          ├── TDID         C(004)    Text-ID
          ├── TDSPRAS      C(002)    Language
          ├── TDOBJEKT     C(010)    Textobject
          ├── TDNAME       C(018)    Name
          ├── TDFORMSAT    C(002)    Format-column
          └── TDLINE       C(132)    Text-line
```

Figure 6.5: Long text — source fields

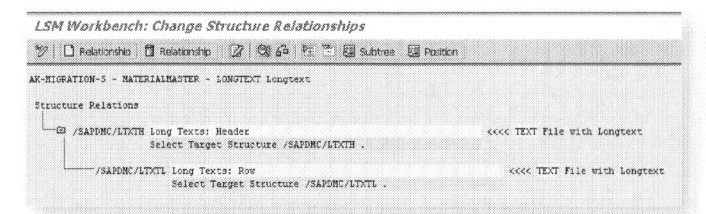

Figure 6.6: Long text — structure relationships

6.4 Long Text — Field Mapping

For our example, due to the good preparation of the source file (see Figure 6.3), a 1:1 field mapping is possible, as illustrated below (see Figure 6.7 and Figure 6.8).

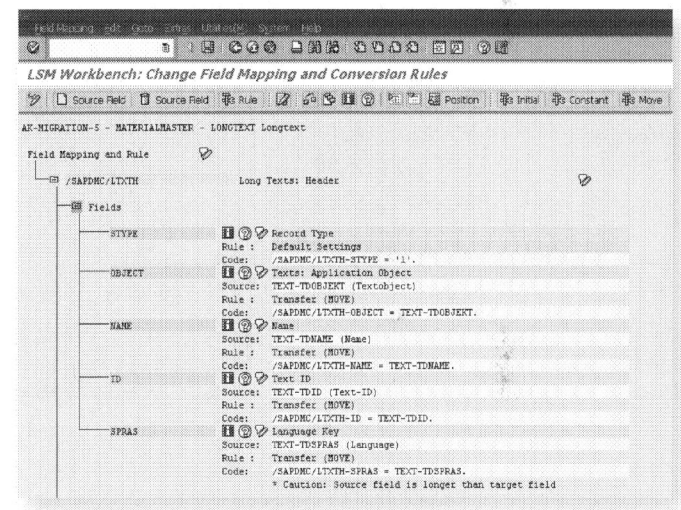

Figure 6.7: Long text — field mapping 1

LONG TEXTS

```
 Field Mapping  Edit  Goto  Extras  Utilities(M)  System  Help
 ⊘                    ▾  ◁ 🖫 | ✦ ✪ ✪ | 🗎 🛗 🛗 | 🏵 🏵 🏵 🏵 | 🖼 🖫 | ⓘ 🖫

 LSM Workbench: Change Field Mapping and Conversion Rules
 🗐 | 🗋 Source Field  🗋 Source Field  🏗 Rule | 🖉 | 🗗 🗘 🖫 ⓘ | 🛗 🛗 🗎 Position | 🏗 Initial  🏗

 AK-MIGRATION-5 - MATERIALMASTER - LONGTEXT Longtext

 Field Mapping and Rule      ⌾
   └─🗀 /SAPDMC/LTXTH              Long Texts: Header
      ┌─🗒 Fields
      └─🗀 /SAPDMC/LTXTL           Long Texts: Row
           └─🗒 Fields
                ├─STYPE            🖫 ⓘ 🗘 Record Type
                │                  Rule : Default Settings
                │                  Code:   /SAPDMC/LTXTL-STYPE = '2'.
                ├─TEXTFORMAT       🖫 ⓘ 🗘 Tag column
                │                  Source: TEXT-TDFORMSAT (Format-column)
                │                  Rule :  Transfer (MOVE)
                │                  Code:   /SAPDMC/LTXTL-TEXTFORMAT = TEXT-TDFORMSAT.
                └─TEXTLINE         🖫 ⓘ 🗘 Text Line
```

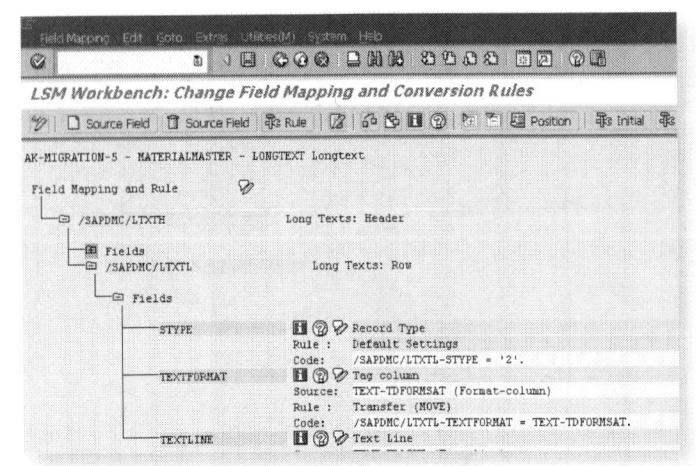

Figure 6.8: Long text — field mapping 2

If we leave these settings in the field mapping as they are, for each text line a text header is created. It is not the case that three lines of inspection text (Text ID PRUE) are created; rather, the first line is continually overwritten. To prevent this, we have to intervene and use a method of functions for advanced users described in Section 8.3: the global function PROCESSING TIMES.

Click the DISPLAY VARIANT button (🗗) and select PROCESSING TIMES. Additional lines are now displayed. At the end of each target structure, the text _END_OF_RECORD appears (see Figure 6.9). Select this instruction at the end of the structure LONG TEXTS: HEADER (/SAPDMC/LTXTH) by double-clicking it. This takes you to the ABAP Editor. There you change the standard assignment to ON_CHANGE_TRANSFER_RECORD (see Figure 6.9). This ABAP instruction has the effect that the text header is only transferred if it has changed compared to the previous entry. Each text line is now written individually (see Figure 6.10).

134

LONG TEXTS

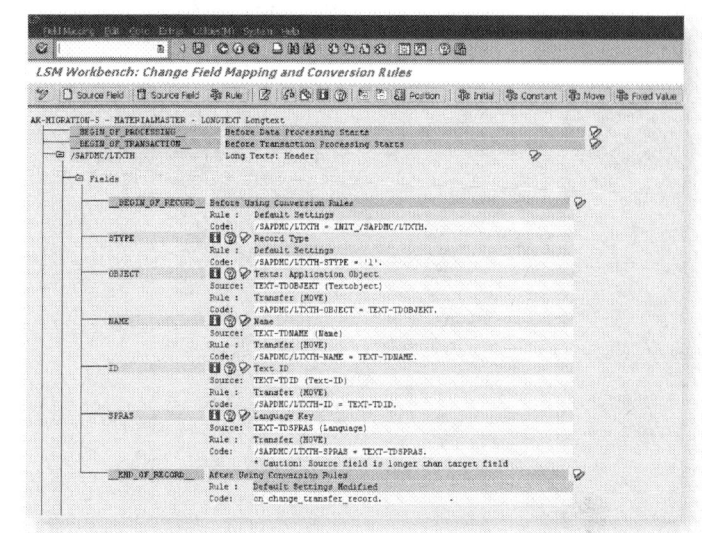

Figure 6.9: Global functions

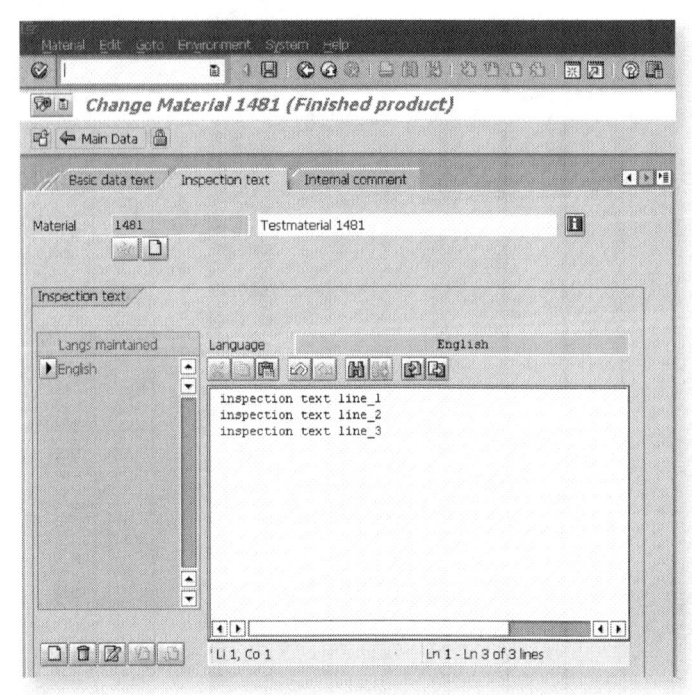

Figure 6.10: Multiple line inspection text

6.5 Final Process Steps for Transferring Long Texts

We do not have to maintain fixed values, translations, and user-defined routines in this example, which means that we can go straight to SPECIFY FILES. In our case, the file is an input file (longtext.txt) that is stored on the frontend PC (for the file content, see Figure 6.3). After importing and converting the files, you can display them on the screen (see Figure 6.11). In Section 6.4 we executed an ABAP instruction for the three-line inspection text — the illustration shows that as a result, only one header line has been created for this text.

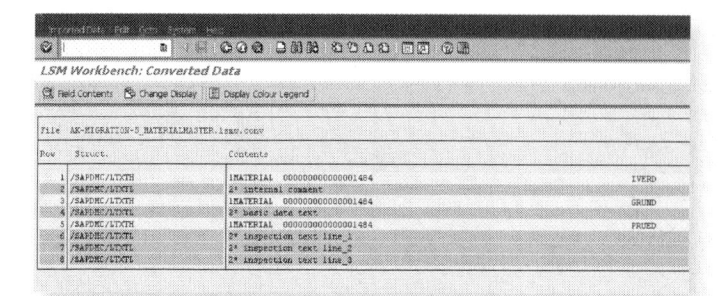

Figure 6.11: Long text — converted data

You can now start the direct input program. It imports the texts and writes them directly to the database.

7 Transporting Projects

Data for an LSMW project can be transported via SAP Transport Management and via download and upload.

Note that the default settings for the IDoc inbound processing are not transported. You have to create these again in each client and each SAP system for each LSMW project.

7.1 Transport via Change Request

You can create an SAP change request, which contains all information for an LSMW project, as follows:

1. Navigate to the LSM Workbench initial screen (see Figure 3.4) and enter all the project data.

2. Choose EXTRAS • CREATE CHANGE REQUEST.

3. Create a new request with a name or select an existing change request.

4. Save the entries.

You can now export or re-import the change request with the usual tools of SAP Change and Transport Management. An advantage of transporting the LSMW data in this way is that in SAP Change and Transport Management, you can see at any time who transported what to where and when they transported it.

> **Transporting LSMW Projects Using Change Requests**
>
> During the **export** of the transport request, the current status of the project and not the status at the time of creation of the transport request is transferred. Therefore, you must make sure that the project has the correct status at the time of the transport and is not changed after the creation of the transport request.
>
> During the **import** of a change request, the entire project is deleted in the target system first and then recreated.

7.2 Exporting Projects

When you want to go live with the LSMW project created in the test system, you have to export it first.

To do this, on the initial screen (see Figure 2.3), click EXTRAS • EXPORT PROJECT. In the dialog box that opens, select the project to be exported. The structure tree for the project is then displayed (see Figure 7.1). Using SELECT/DESELECT (![icon]), you can then select or deselect the parts to be transferred and then EXPORT (![icon]) them. In the dialog box that opens, enter the name and path of the text file to be created and confirm the entry. All specified elements (mapping and set of rules) are then exported with the relevant documentation.

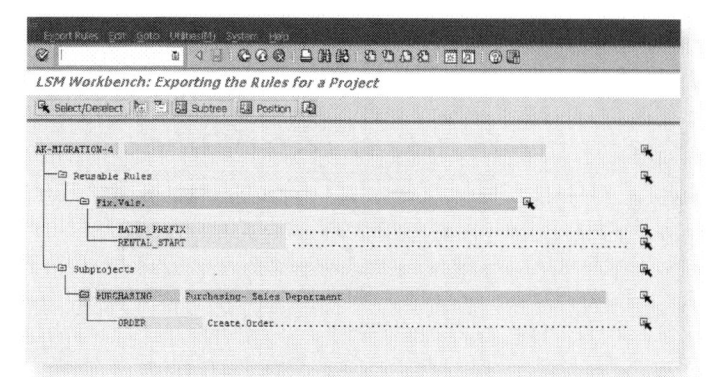

Figure 7.1: Exporting projects

7.3 Importing Projects

You can import the exported mapping with the set of rules into another SAP system.

Again, the starting point is the initial screen from Figure 2.3. This time, choose LSMW • EXTRAS • IMPORT PROJECT. The system prompts you to enter the name and path of the text file to be imported. Once you have entered and confirmed this information, the file is read to SAP and the content analyzed. After successful completion of the analysis, you receive an overview of the subprojects and objects determined in a matching format, as shown in Figure 7.1 for projects to be exported. You can select and deselect which objects are to be imported. If data with the same name already exists for this project, this data is indicated with a green checkmark. This data will be overwritten by the import. You can prevent an existing project in the target system from being overwritten by using the function IMPORT UNDER ANOTHER NAME ( ).

If the message ERROR WHEN UPLOADING FILE appears during the import, check whether the directory you have specified exists and whether you have authorization to write to it.

8 Additional Information

With the basic principles for working with the LSM Workbench described so far, you will already be able to perform a large part of the migration work. In addition, there are a series of measures for modifying the set of rules and the data conversion program of a project.

For advanced LSMW users who want to go into the topic in more depth, the functions described below can be very interesting. However, this chapter will provide all interested readers with information that makes working with LSMW easier.

I already gave you a brief glimpse of the extended LSMW functions with the migration of long texts in Section 6.4, for example. Below I will briefly explain the *periodic data transfer* addressed in Section 3.2.

8.1 Periodic Data Transfer

With this form of data transfer, the data is not imported once from a legacy system, but at regular intervals from a source system. The following prerequisites must be fulfilled:

- ▶ The corresponding LSMW object has been created completely and successfully tested.

- ▶ At regular intervals, the source system provides the required file(s) on the application server of the target system.

- ▶ The LSMW object only accesses the files of the application server. (Files on the frontend cannot be read during a periodic data transfer that takes place in the background.)

- ▶ Furthermore, in the process step MAINTAIN OBJECT ATTRIBUTES, the indicator for the periodic data transfer must be set (see Figure 3.6). This ensures that at the end of the navigation screen (see Figure 3.4), an additional process step is displayed: Frame Program for Periodic Data Transfer. This framework program, with the name /SAPDMC/SAP_LSMW_INTERFACE, is an additional program to the LSMW and performs the periodic data transfer in the following steps:

  1. Read in data
  2. Convert data
  3. Import data

You can schedule the framework program according to your requirements. Figure 8.1 to Figure 8.3 show the numerous selection parameters of the program. Create a variant for the program and schedule the corresponding job periodically. You can do this using transaction SM36 (alternatively: SYSTEM • JOBS • JOB DEFINITION), or using the job scheduling software available in your system (for example, UC4).

You can also enter variants for the read and the conversion program respectively, as well as, if used, for the batch input and direct input program. You have to define these beforehand.

ADDITIONAL INFORMATION

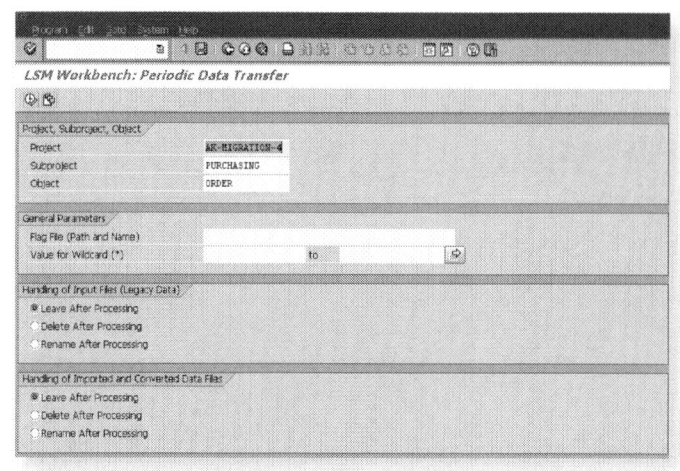

Figure 8.1: Program for periodic data transfer 1

Figure 8.2: Program for periodic data transfer 2

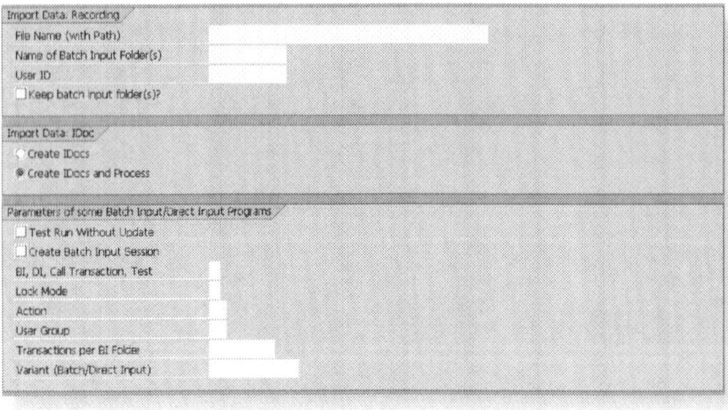

Figure 8.3: Program for periodic data transfer 3

In Figure 8.1, under General Parameters, you can specify a *flag file*. This entry is optional. A flag file establishes a *handshake* between the source and target systems to avoid data being imported twice by mistake. This handshake consists of the following steps:

1. The framework program for the periodic data transfer (/SAPDMC/SAP_LSMW_INTERFACE) checks whether the flag file specified is available. Processing is only started if it is available.

2. After completion of the entire processing, the program /SAPDMC/SAP_LSMW_INTERFACE deletes the flag file.

3. The "data-supplying" application should act complementary to this, that is, before new transfer files are provided, there should be a check to determine whether the flag file is available. If the flag file is available, the processing is terminated. Otherwise the program creates the files to be read in the source system and creates the flag file.

The contents of the flag file are irrelevant. The file can even be empty. The system only checks whether the file is available — not what it contains.

> **Input Parameters for Direct and BTCI Programs**
>
> Note that some of the standard direct or batch input programs use additional input parameters. You can find these at the end of the selection parameter overview for program /SAP-DMC/SAP_LSMW_INTERFACE (see Figure 8.3).

Table 8.1 shows an overview of the parameters used by each standard program.

Program	Short Description	Test Run without Update	Batch Input Creation	BI, DI, Call Transaction, Test	Locking Mode	Procedure	User Group
RAALTD01	Legacy Data Transfer Program - Asset Accounting	X					
RAALTD11	Direct Data Import - Asset Accounting	X					
RCCLBI 01	Batch Input: Create Classes		X				
RCCLBI 02	Batch Input: Create Classification Data		X				
RCCLBI 03	Maintain Classification Data		X				
RCCTBI 01	Batch Input: Create Characteristics		X				
RCSBI 010	Create BOMs using Batch Input		X				
RCSBI 020	Change BOMs using Batch Input		X				
RCSBI 030	Create Variant BOMs using Batch Input		X				
RCSBI 040	Create BOMs with All Long Texts using Batch Input		X				
RCVBI 010	Create Document Info Records via Batch Input		X				
RFBI BL00	Batch Input Documents			X			
RHALTD00	Legacy Data Transfer Personnel Planning Data			X			
RLBEST00	Batch Input for Init.Entry of Stock Data	X					
RLPLAT00	Legacy Data Transfer Storage Bin	X					
RMDATI ND	Transfer Material Master Data by Direct Input				X		
RPUSTD00	Transfer Master Data from Old HR System					X	X

Table 8.1: Programs and parameters

8.2 Global Functions and Variables

The LSM Workbench provides a series of functions and variables that you can use at any point in the ABAP code.

You can get an overview of the global functions in the process step MAINTAIN FIELD MAPPING AND CONVERSION RULES (see Figure 3.19) by double-clicking one of the target fields to switch to the ABAP code. There, choose INSERT • GLOBAL FUNCTIONS to get the overview of available functions shown in Figure 8.4.

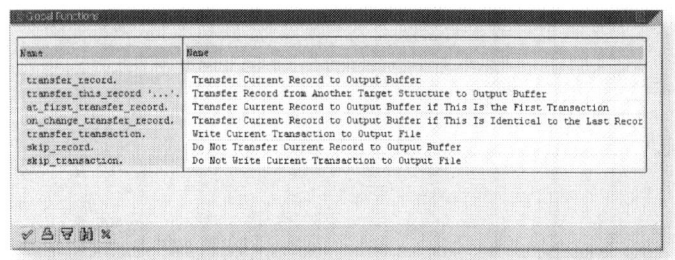

Name	Name
transfer_record.	Transfer Current Record to Output Buffer
transfer_this_record '...'.	Transfer Record from Another Target Structure to Output Buffer
at_first_transfer_record.	Transfer Current Record to Output Buffer if This Is the First Transaction
on_change_transfer_record.	Transfer Current Record to Output Buffer if This Is Identical to the Last Record
transfer_transaction.	Write Current Transaction to Output File
skip_record.	Do Not Transfer Current Record to Output Buffer
skip_transaction.	Do Not Write Current Transaction to Output File

Figure 8.4: Global functions

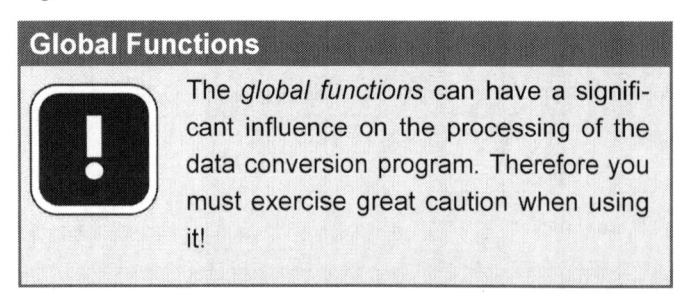

Global Functions

The *global functions* can have a significant influence on the processing of the data conversion program. Therefore you must exercise great caution when using it!

To select the *global variables*, proceed in the same way as for the global functions. This time, in the code, choose INSERT • GLOBAL VARIABLES to display the global variables that can be used in your ABAP code (see Figure 8.5).

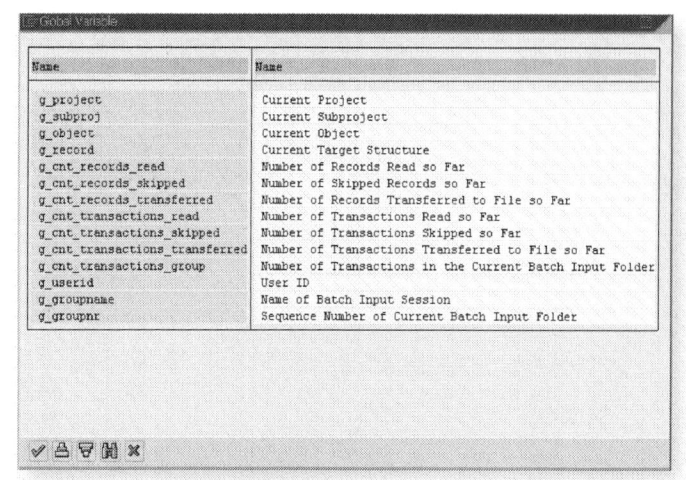

Name	Name
g_project	Current Project
g_subproj	Current Subproject
g_object	Current Object
g_record	Current Target Structure
g_cnt_records_read	Number of Records Read so Far
g_cnt_records_skipped	Number of Skipped Records so Far
g_cnt_records_transferred	Number of Records Transferred to File so Far
g_cnt_transactions_read	Number of Transactions Read so Far
g_cnt_transactions_skipped	Number of Transactions Skipped so Far
g_cnt_transactions_transferred	Number of Transactions Transferred to File so Far
g_cnt_transactions_group	Number of Transactions in the Current Batch Input Folder
g_userid	User ID
g_groupname	Name of Batch Input Session
g_groupnr	Sequence Number of Current Batch Input Folder

Figure 8.5: Global variables

8.3 Display Variants and Processing Times

The function MAINTAIN FIELD MAPPING AND CONVERSION RULES (see Figure 3.19) is of particular benefit for advanced users who want to modify the field mapping. You can use it to select which information to display on the screen. To do this, click DISPLAY VARIANT ( ). The dialog box shown in Figure 8.6 appears.

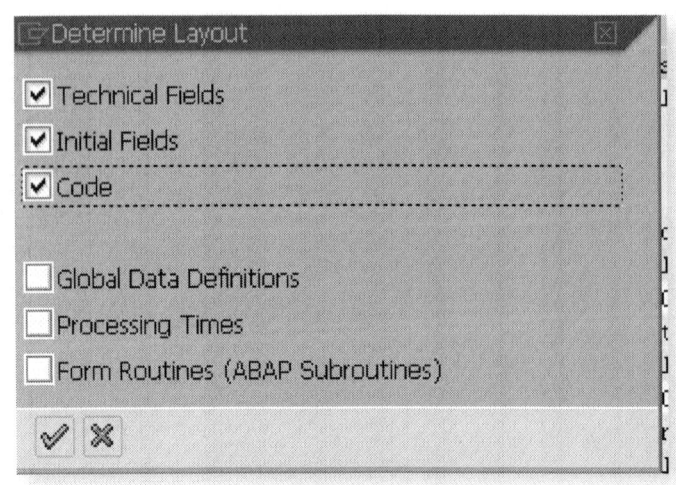

Figure 8.6: Determining display variants

The selection of the corresponding field determines which information is displayed. The following is an explanation of the given selection fields and their meaning.

▶ Technical Fields

These are target fields for which the LSM Workbench proposes a conversion rule. You generally do not have to make any changes here.

▶ Initial Fields

Neither a source field nor a conversion rule has been assigned to these fields. To compress the display, it can be useful to hide these fields after completing the field mapping.

▶ Code

If you select this field, the existing ABAP code is displayed.

▶ Global Data Definitions

You use this field to display the additional object _GLOBAL_DATA_. There you can store definitions and declarations that are available in the entire conversion program (see Figure 8.7).

▶ Processing Times

If you select PROCESSING TIMES, you can insert your own code for certain processing times. Additional objects are displayed, similarly to the situation for GLOBAL DATA DEFINITIONS.

Table 8.2 shows the processing times and global data definitions displayed.

Processing time	Description
__BEGIN_OF_PROCESSING__	Before the start of data processing
__END_OF_PROCESSING__	After the end of data processing
__BEGIN_OF_TRANSACTION__	Before the start of transaction processing
__END_OF_TRANSACTION__	After the end of transaction processing. Default assignment: Transfer_transaction.
__BEGIN_OF_RECORD__	Before application of the conversion rules to a source structure. The structure is initialized as the default assignment
__END_OF_RECORD	After application of the conversion rules to a source structure. Default assignment: Transfer_record

Table 8.2: Processing times

▶ Form Routines (ABAP Subroutines)

You can also define ABAP subroutines that you want to use in your own code for the field mapping. You can do this by selecting the display variant FORM ROUTINES. Then, at the end of the field mapping, the label _FORM_ROUTINES is displayed (see Figure 8.7), and here you can integrate the form routines.

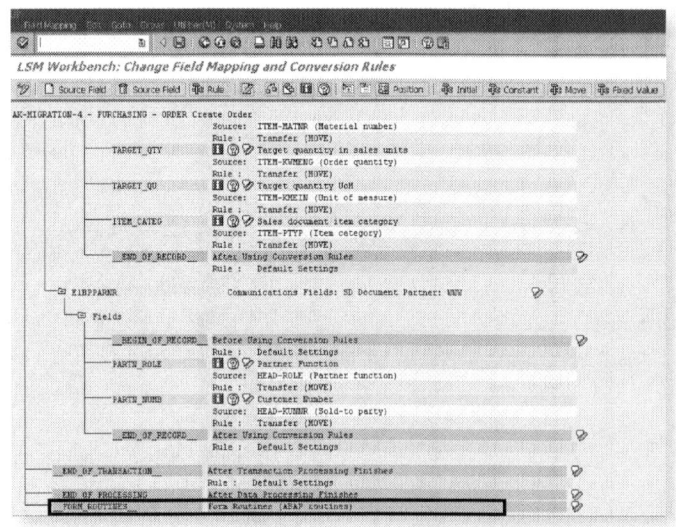

Figure 8.7: Display variants in the field mapping

8.4 Suppressing Data Records

If you do not want to migrate certain data records from your legacy system to SAP, you can filter these out of the input file or use SKIP_RECORD in the LSM Workbench to skip them. I will explain the latter option here.

In change mode, navigate to the process step MAINTAIN FIELD MAPPING AND CONVERSION RULES. Select the field whose condition is to be checked and integrate the following ABAP instruction:

> IF <condition>.
>
> > skip_record.
>
> ENDIF.

Together with the corresponding condition, the function SKIP_RECORD must be called up in every structure that is not to be transferred. This suppresses the transfer of the corresponding record to the output file.

8.5 Creating Additional Data Records

Conversely, you may want to create one or more additional target records from one source record. Of course you can prepare the input file(s)—for example, in Excel—such that you create a separate source record for each target record. However, it is much easier to duplicate data records using the LSMW and form routine TRANSFER_RECORD.

Again, you do this in the process step MAINTAIN FIELD MAPPING AND CONVERSION RULES. At the processing time _End_ of_Record, the instruction TRANSFER_RECORD triggers the transfer of the corresponding data record as standard. You could duplicate the data record here.

I will explain this using our example from Chapter 3 — the migration of debitors with corresponding contact persons. Imagine that instead of receiving two source files (one with the debitor header information and one with the contact partners), everything is stored in one file. Thus, for each debitor, you have multiple contact persons in one line (see

Figure 8.8) and have to create one record in the structure BKNVK for each. Converting one source file into multiple files could be time-consuming and prone to error. In contrast, the creation of multiple records in LSMW is very easy.

debitor	country	name	place	postal code	phone	street	First Name2	Names	Phone1	First Name2	Name2	Phone2
200000	GER	Udo Neureich	Gunzenhausen	91710	09831-45678	Goldanger 99	Lisa	Lasowich	09831-45678	Peer	Früher	09831-45680
210000	GER	Maria Magredit	Dresden	04244	04442 123000	Flowerstreet 8	Ludwig	Verkauf was	098-787878	Lieschen	Machwas	098-787088
240000	USA	Billy Buties AG	Chicago, IL	60637	773-702-7777	Michigan Avenue 444	Ute	Sommer	0987-45677	Beate	Fragmichnicht	0987-45666
270000	USA	Flower Power Shop	Chicago, IL	60630	773-752-7000	East 60th Street	Niklas	Winter	066-99999	Joachim	Sales	066-99888

Figure 8.8: Input file with contact persons

Maintain the source fields as shown in Figure 8.9. The data of the first contact person is transferred as normal in the structure BKNVK (see Figure 8.10 upper part). To create a new record with the data of the second contact person, change the default assignment at the processing time _END_OF_RECORD of the structure BKNVK as shown in Figure 8.10 (lower part). The following happens: with the first TRANSFER_RECORD, the data record for the first contact person is transferred. Then the BKNVK record is initialized using the instruction INIT_BKNVK. The data for the second contact person is now filled and, via TRANSFER_RECORD, an additional data record is transferred to the input file for the batch or direct input program.

ADDITIONAL INFORMATION

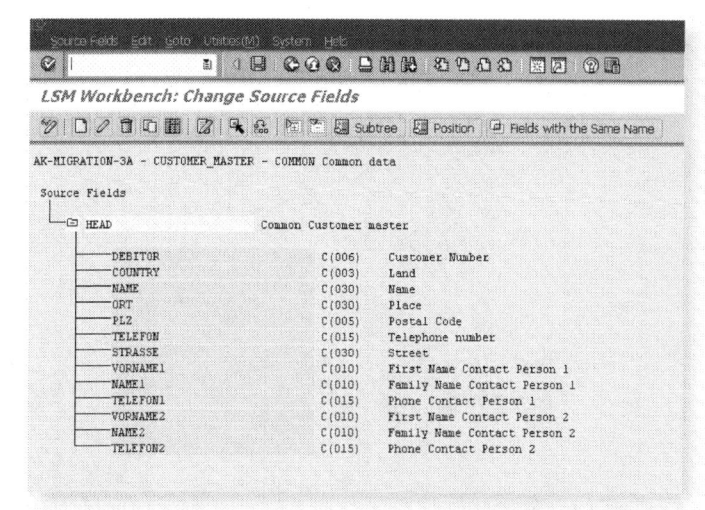

```
LSM Workbench: Change Source Fields

AK-MIGRATION-3A - CUSTOMER_MASTER - COMMON Common data

Source Fields

  HEAD                        Common Customer master
    DEBITOR             C(006)    Customer Number
    COUNTRY             C(003)    Land
    NAME                C(030)    Name
    ORT                 C(030)    Place
    PLZ                 C(005)    Postal Code
    TELEFON             C(015)    Telephone number
    STRASSE             C(030)    Street
    VORNAME1            C(010)    First Name Contact Person 1
    NAME1               C(010)    Family Name Contact Person 1
    TELEFON1            C(015)    Phone Contact Person 1
    VORNAME2            C(010)    First Name Contact Person 2
    NAME2               C(010)    Family Name Contact Person 2
    TELEFON2            C(015)    Phone Contact Person 2
```

Figure 8.9: Customer master source fields with contact persons

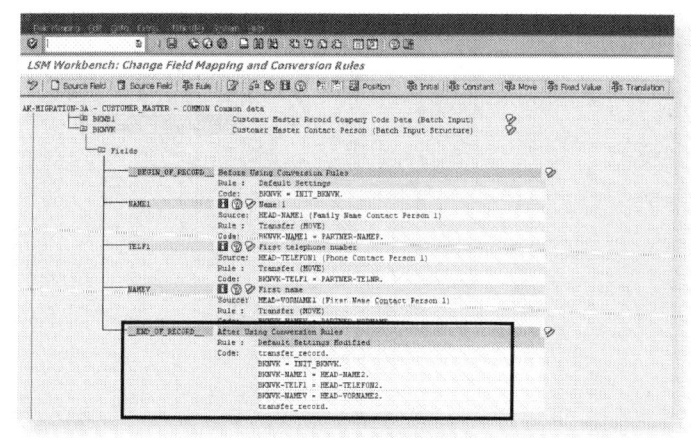

```
LSM Workbench: Change Field Mapping and Conversion Rules

AK-MIGRATION-3A - CUSTOMER_MASTER - COMMON Common data
  BKN01        Customer Master Record Company Code Data (Batch Input)
  BKNVK        Customer Master Contact Person (Batch Input Structure)

    Fields
      BEGIN_OF_RECORD  Before Using Conversion Rules
                       Rule : Default Settings
                       Code:  BKNVK = INIT_BKNVK.
      NAME1            Name 1
                       Source: HEAD-NAME1 (Family Name Contact Person 1)
                       Rule :  Transfer (MOVE)
                       Code:   BKNVK-NAME1 = PARTNER-NAMEP.
      TELF1            First telephone number
                       Source: HEAD-TELEFON1 (Phone Contact Person 1)
                       Rule :  Transfer (MOVE)
                       Code:   BKNVK-TELF1 = PARTNER-TELNR.
      NAMEV            First name
                       Source: HEAD-VORNAME1 (First Name Contact Person 1)
                       Rule :  Transfer (MOVE)

      END_OF_RECORD    After Using Conversion Rules
                       Rule :  Default Settings Modified
                       Code:   transfer_record.
                               BKNVK = INIT_BKNVK.
                               BKNVK-NAME1 = HEAD-NAME2.
                               BKNVK-TELF1 = HEAD-TELEFON2.
                               BKNVK-NAMEV = HEAD-VORNAME2.
                               transfer_record.
```

Figure 8.10: Creating additional data records

155

9 Closing Words

The aim of this book was to provide a clear and understandable complete overview of all important topics for the powerful LSMW tool.

After working through the explanations, beginners should be able to create their own LSM Workbench projects or change or extend existing projects to meet their requirements. The book provides experienced LSMW users with a compact reference work that answers a lot of their questions in this area.

If you wish to examine this topic in more depth, the most up-to-date information is always available on SAP Service Marketplace under *https://service.sap.com/lsmw*.

Our Solution for Business Customers:

The SAP eBook Library

Mobile, flexible, and practical

Learn more at:

http://library.espresso-tutorials.com

espresso tutorials

Our newsletter will inform you about new publications and exclusive free downloads.

Subscribe today at
http://newsletter.espresso-tutorials.com!

A The Author

Antje Kunz studied Information Processing at the Technical University of Dresden and has been employed in the SAP environment for 20 years. Starting as a systems analyst, and progressing through the roles of team and project lead, as well as manager, to her current employment as a freelance IT consultant, Antje has been involved in various fields and positions in the SAP environment.

In multiple international SAP rollouts, Antje has been responsible for data migration, thus enabling her to gather extensive experience with LSMW.

B Index

A

ABAP 30, 136
ABAP code 50, 62, 148, 150
ABAP instruction 153
ABAP subroutines 152
Action log 27
Administration 21
Authorization concept 14
Automatic value collector 61

B

BAPI 11, 12, 48, 49, 107, 108, 116
BAPI Explorer 116
BAPI import technology 114
BAPI method 117
Batch input 11, 12, 29, 32, 42, 77, 79, 80, 82
BTCI 11, 79, 102
BTCI session 102, 104
Business Application Programming Interface 108
Business Framework 108
Business method 115
Business object 115

C

Change log 22, 27
Change mode 28
Code 150, 151, 152
Concatenation 50
Control record 42
Conversion rules 42
Customizing 14

D

Data conversion 12
Data conversion file 62
Data Dictionary 41, 46
Data migration 12
Data migration object 16
Data transfer 29
Data Transfer Center 11
Direct input 11, 12, 29, 32, 42, 48, 49
Display variant 149
Dynpro 81

E

Existing system 29

F

Field mapping 42, 44, 48, 134, 152
File port 110
Fixed value 21, 27
Flag file 146
Form routine 153
Framework program 144

G

Global data definitions 151
Global functions 147
Global variables 147, 148

I

IDoc 11, 12, 32, 48, 49, 107, 108, 124
Import method 28, 29, 31, 87
Import project 141
Import technology 31, 32, 39, 107
Initial fields 150
Intermediate document 108

K

Key field 38

L

Legacy data 64
Legacy file 104
Legacy system 12, 29
Legacy System Migration Workbench 15
Long text 127
LSMW 11
LSMW administration area 22
LSMW initial screen 16, 19
LSMW main menu 33
LSM Workbench 11, 12, 16, 24
LSMW user guidance 24

M

MASS 12
Mass change transaction 12
Mass update 11
Migration 12, 23
Migration object 17
Migration project 17, 24
Migration test 37

N

New implementation 12

O

Object type 28
OK code 81, 104

P

Partner number 112
Partner status 112
Partner type 112
Periodic data transfer 143
Port 110
Prefix 49
Processing time 149, 151
Project name 17

R

Recording 48, 87, 88, 90, 95, 98
Recording technology 32
Reusable rules 21, 27

S

SAP required field 14
SAP standard method 12
SAP Transport Management 139
Screen 93
Selection parameter 73
Source field 35, 37, 38, 44, 45, 50, 69, 73
Source record 153
Source structure 11, 33, 35, 38, 65, 83, 99
Source system 23
Standard batch 48
Standard interface 32
Structure relationship 39, 40, 41, 83
Suffix 49

T

Target field 44, 46, 48
Target structure 39, 83
Technical fields 150
Text header 134
Text line 134
Text pool 127
Transaction 14, 15, 32, 78, 90, 93, 97, 102, 114, 115, 126, 144
Transfer rule 44, 45
Translation 14, 21, 27, 49, 58, 59, 60, 61
Translation rules 58

U

User-defined routine 50
User ID 102
User menu 25
User-specific fields 12

W

Welcome screen 16
Wildcard 67, 73

X

XD99 12
X FIELD 50
XK99 12

C Disclaimer

This publication contains references to the products of SAP SE.

SAP, R/3, SAP NetWeaver, Duet, PartnerEdge, ByDesign, SAP BusinessObjects Explorer, StreamWork, and other SAP products and services mentioned herein as well as their respective logos are trademarks or registered trademarks of SAP AG in Germany and other countries.

BusinessObjects and the BusinessObjects logo, BusinessObjects, Crystal Reports, Crystal Decisions, Web Intelligence, Xcelsius, and other BusinessObjects products and services mentioned herein as well as their respective logos are trademarks or registered trademarks of BusinessObjects Software Ltd. BusinessObjects is an SAP company.

Sybase and Adaptive Server, iAnywhere, Sybase 365, SQL Anywhere, and other Sybase products and services mentioned herein as well as their respective logos are trademarks or registered trademarks of Sybase, Inc. Sybase is an SAP company.

SAP AG is neither the author nor the publisher of this publication and is not responsible for its content. SAP Group shall not be liable for errors or omissions with respect to the materials. The only warranties for SAP Group products and services are those that are set forth in the express warranty statements accompanying such products and services, if any. Nothing herein should be construed as constituting an additional warranty.

More Books from Espresso Tutorials

Boris Rubarth:

First Steps in ABAP®

- ▶ Step-by-Step instructions for beginners
- ▶ Comprehensive descriptions and code examples
- ▶ A guide to create your first ABAP application

http://5015.espresso-tutorials.com

Tanya Duncan:

The Essential SAP® Career Guide

- ▶ How to find a job with SAP
- ▶ Creating a stand-out SAP resume
- ▶ Choosing the right SAP module and how to develop skills in other modules

http://5012.espresso-tutorials.com

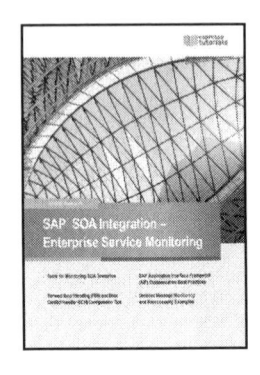

Michal Krawczyk:

SAP® SOA – Enterprise Service Monitoring

- ▶ Tools for Monitoring SOA Scenarios
- ▶ Forward Error Handling (FEH) and Error Conflict Handler (ECH) Configuration Tips
- ▶ SAP Application Interface Framework (AIF) Customization Best Practices

http://5077.espresso-tutorials.com

Darren Hague:

Universal Worklist with SAP® NetWeaver Portal

- ▶ Standard UWL configuration: Connecting SAP systems, items in the UWL, changing the basic look
- ▶ Customizing UWL: Custom views, custom work item handlers
- ▶ Integrating other types of workflow: Ad-hoc workflow, publishing workflow, 3rd party workflow

http://5076.espresso-tutorials.com

Janet Salmon & Ulrich Schlüter:

SAP® HANA for ERP Financials

- **Understanding the basics of SAP HANA**
- **Examining already existing HANA applications in SAP Financials**
- **Understanding the concept behind the Financials Add-on**

http://5092.espresso-tutorials.com

Made in the USA
Lexington, KY
01 March 2019